MAKING SPACE FOR MORMON THOUGHT AND CULTURE

Eugene England

# MAKING SPACE FOR MORMON THOUGHT AND CULTURE

## THE ENDURING INFLUENCE OF EUGENE ENGLAND

EDITED BY
ROBERT A. REES &
BRENT RUSHFORTH

SIGNATURE BOOKS | 2025 | SALT LAKE CITY

*For*
*Katherine, Jody, Mark, Jennifer, Rebecca & Jane*
*In and through whom the world continues to see and be blessed by their father.*

"My father gave me the greatest gift anyone could give another person: He believed in me." — Jim Valvano

"There are two gifts a father can give his children. One is roots. The other is wings."



Join our mailing list at signaturebooks.com for details on events and related titles we think you'll enjoy.

Cover photo by John Snyder
Design by Jason Francis

FIRST EDITION | 2025

Paperback ISBN: 978-1-56085-523-1
Ebook ISBN: 978-1-56085-504-0

# Contents

# Foreword

Those of us whose lives were changed by Gene England were thrilled by the recent publication of critically acclaimed and award-winning biographies written by two of the finest scholars in the Latter-day Saint tradition and published by two highly regarded university presses: Terryl Givens's *Stretching the Heavens: The Life of Eugene England and the Crisis of Modern Mormonism* (University of North Carolina Press, 2021) and Kristine Haglund's *Eugene England: A Mormon Liberal* (University of Illinois Press, 2021). Both are indispensable studies of a man who had a profound impact on Latter-day Saint culture during a time of transformation within the church. Each captures vital elements of that story.

But no single biography or even two can paint more than a partial portrait of the influence of a person so consequential as Gene. The editors of this volume seek to add a few brush strokes to that portrait through the voices of some of the many people whose faith in Christ and commitment to the Church of Jesus Christ of Latter-day Saints were strengthened by Gene. He had that effect on us.

Robert Rees's friendship with Gene began in 1966 with the publication of *Dialogue: A Journal of Mormon Thought*, which led to his becoming the second editor of the journal, co-editing *The Reader's Book of Mormon* (2008) with Gene, and editing a tribute to Gene, *"Proving Contraries": A Collection of Writings in Honor of Eugene England* (2005). Brent Rushforth first met Gene while a student at Stanford in the 1960s and was present with Gene at the creation of *Dialogue*. For each of us, Gene fanned the fires of our faith. His commitment to the church, his profound belief that its origins are divine and that it is led today by apostles and prophets called by Christ, strengthened our resolve to help the church fulfill its mission in the world.

We offer this collection of remembrances of how Gene changed lives with the hope that those who study his life will see that he was, first and foremost, a devoted disciple of Christ who "labor[ed] diligently to write, to persuade [others] to believe in Christ, and to be reconciled to God … [and] look forward unto that life which is in Christ." (2 Ne. 25:23, 27)

Robert A. Rees
Brent Rushforth

# Introduction
# The Lengthened Shadow of Eugene England

**ROBERT A. REES AND BRENT RUSHFORTH**

Emerson observed that "every great institution is the lengthened shadow of one man" (it's unlikely a nineteenth-century man would have considered adding "woman" to that aphorism!). We do not assert that Mormon studies could be seen entirely as the lengthened shadow of Eugene England; nonetheless, it is hard to imagine another scholar/teacher/disciple over the past seventy years who is considered as influential as Gene, or one whose shadow has been as long and as long-lasting as his. While some Latter-day Saints, because of position and power, could be said to have had a wider and longer influence on the general Latter-day Saint community, history is likely to show that Gene's courage, innovation, imagination, and pure Christian discipleship will outlast those of most of his Latter-day Saint contemporaries.

By his use of "shadow," which today we tend to associate with the darker side of our natures, we believe Emerson intended that we consider how light makes shadow possible. Through the Light of Christ—the birthright of all God's children—we are blessed to choose the more luminous and radiant light of the Holy Ghost, which intensifies and magnifies our light and the shadow it makes possible. As these brief remembrances and tributes celebrate, that radiance was evident: in Gene's teaching, in his writing of both prose and poetry (especially the personal essay which he prized and perfected), in his imaginative and innovative organizing (e.g., *Dialogue*, The Association of Mormon Letters, Food for Poland, the Mormon Studies Program at UVU, etc.), in his graceful and benevolent service to others, in his (and Charlotte's) bountiful and indiscriminate hospitality, and perhaps especially in those qualities Wordsworth spoke of as the "best portion of a good man's life ... his little, nameless, unremembered acts of kindness and of love." In relation to Gene, this collection reveals that, not only are those acts not "unremembered," but they are truly and gratefully remembered by many who came within the wide circle of his influence.

## TEACHER

Some of the most indelible remembrances of Gene are from his students at the Stanford and University of Utah Institutes of Religion, and in college classrooms at St. Olaf's College, BYU, and Utah Valley State University, as well as those who sat at his feet in the numerous firesides and special lectures he gave over the years. Many testify that he was the best teacher they ever had.

Connie Bennion remembers being invited by Gene to a fireside he gave at Stanford: "That is one of the moments when my life took a new direction and became filled with new meaning. This first meeting of the Englands marked the beginning of a lifelong friendship with Gene and Charlotte. For me, Gene's name has become synonymous with 'teacher.' The gifts he has added to my mind, heart, and spirit are too large to be measured and too meaningful to imagine living without."

The classroom wasn't the only place where Gene was a master teacher. Thomas Griffith recalls an occasion when Gene invited him and his three children for a conversation in the BYU faculty lounge: "There, for the next hour, Gene directed the conversation not to me but to my teenaged children. I sat back and watched a great teacher talk to my children. I watched him model love, genuine interest, and empathy. At times I had to pinch myself. Here was the man most responsible for the fire of my adult faith and commitment to the church teaching the children I loved more than life, and I knew that he knew what was at stake. It doesn't get any better than that." Susan Gong remembers specific lessons: "Gene was a master teacher. More than forty years later, I still remember his lectures on a variety of topics. No matter how obscure the texts, he succeeded in making them relevant and interesting to his freshmen students."

As a participant in one of Gene's study abroad classes in England, Rosalynde Welch remembers Gene taking his students to a performance of Shakespeare's *King Lear*, which, as always, caused him to weep over the last meeting between Lear and Cordelia. Welch summarizes: "Unusually, Gene's trust in a spiritual otherworld seemed only to hone his appetite for this world, of which his London was surely the premier microcosm. Beauties natural and human, the finest art and entertainment, Indian curries and fish-and-chips: London gave bountifully, and he relished it all, body and spirit. An illuminating line reading of a poem or play brought him the same renewing soul-pleasure. Without sanctimony, Gene brought a quality of attention, specificity, and favor to relationships with his students that I can only describe as blessing."

Warner Woodworth summarizes: "Through his formal and informal teaching, Gene was successful in opening Latter-day Saint college students' minds by helping them explore the expanse of heaven while wrestling with the tensions between the mind and the heart and between the mental and the spiritual elements of Mormonism. I fully believe his life's work helped keep many young Latter-day Saints from leaving the church because, through him, they were able to see that the mind can be integrated with the spirit in an authentic, purposeful life."

### MENTOR

Gene was a mentor to many. As his fellow BYU English teacher, Gideon Burton, remembers in his "Eugene England, Bodhisattva": "When I learned about these saintly beings while studying India's religions, I thought of my former mentor and colleague, Eugene England. He would never characterize himself as someone any better than his sisters or brothers, but to me and many others, he played the role of bodhisattva, a kindly catalyst of enlightenment. And I have needed mentors who are unafraid to have convictions, follow commandments, prize covenants, and live a life of intentional discipleship. This is no easy combination."

### WRITER

Gene was a champion and master of the personal essay, which he felt was the genre most suited to Latter-day Saint experience and expression. Many of the contributors to this volume speak of the influence of such essays as "The Possibility of Dialogue," "The Church Is as True as the Gospel," "The Weeping God of Mormonism," and "That They Might Not Suffer: The Gift of the Atonement." Of the latter, his fellow BYU professor, John Rosenberg, writes: "In the 1966 essay on the atonement … Gene proposes this simple question about Gethsemane: 'If God can have this kind of love for me, who am I to withhold it from myself?' Reading this in 2022, at a time when I experienced the mystery of being generously loved by many without feeling particularly loveable, I nearly jumped from my chair in response to Gene's question. Who am I, indeed?"

Brent Rushforth observes Gene's "The Church Is as True as the Gospel" "has greatly affected my life … Its primary idea is that the structure of the church in putting us together in a framework of mutual caring and service is as important to our learning how to love one another (an essential goal of our mortality) as are the concepts and ideas of our religion." Chad Jones remembers, "In 1985, my faith was flagging. It wasn't doctrine or history that prompted what we now call a faith crisis, but a philosophical alienation from my community." Upon reading Gene's essay "On Finding Truth and God," he recounts, "My half empty cup became half full." Susan Hinkley's words express the sentiments of many: "He wrote hope for me."

### ECCLESIASTICAL LEADER

It is not surprising that those who had the privilege of having Gene as a bishop or branch president experienced the same qualities of intelligence, compassion, imagination, and love that characterized his other roles. Boyd Petersen summarizes what many remember: "Gene was a bishop unlike any other I've had before or since. He was personally involved with each member of the ward."

Greg Reece speaks of his experience of being blessed by Gene's leadership of a small branch in Minnesota: "If he used any power or force to persuade people, it was the power of love ... He knew that through love mighty works were possible, and he worked to keep that the focus. He was a strong advocate for all of us to love one another and demonstrated it powerfully through his example."

### INNOVATOR

Gene was a man of many ideas who saw the imagination as one of the prized gifts of the Spirit. He wasn't content just to imagine a better church and a more just world but worked hard to bring them into fruition through dialogues with himself (the title of one of his books), as well as with God and others. Gene created fellowship by inviting and engaging others into his innovative enterprises, from *Dialogue* to co-edited books, to organizations like the Association of Mormon Letters. In respect to the latter, Lavina Fielding Anderson remembers, "Although we had convened at Gene's suggestion, he sat back listening, letting the group explore the topic. We all agreed that insightful and professional criticism would greatly advance Mormon literature ... After about an hour, Gene glanced at his watch, leaned forward to put his elbows on the table, and said, 'Maureen [Ursenbach Beecher], why don't you chair an executive meeting that will spell out the purposes of good criticism, find a date for an organizational meeting, and oversee the election of officers?' Then he was gone, leaving us rather breathless. Everyone at the meeting eventually became president of the association. Steven [Sondrup] served loyally and efficiently as executive secretary until his retirement from BYU. AML is still thriving to this day."

Gene also used humanitarian projects as an opportunity for fellowship and service. Maxine Hanks recalls, "He was devoted to both his church community and humanitarian causes, like 'Food for Poland.'" Tom Rogers reports, "Because of my knowledge of Polish and my earlier residences in Warsaw and Gdansk, Gene asked me and a few others to join him in promoting his remarkable Food for Poland endeavor after the Solidarity movement's shipyard riots during that country's communist domination."

### HOST

Like Abraham and Sarah, whom the Torah show as keeping the four sides of their tent always open to strangers and guests, Gene and Charlotte's home has always been a perpetual sanctuary for any who needed fellowship, a bed to sleep in, food to eat, and always, in addition to ice cream or other sweets, love and kindness for dessert. In her essay, "The Kindness of Gene and Charlotte," Helen Claire Sievers recalls being in London at a time when Gene and Charlotte were leading a group of BYU students. Not only did the Englands make room for them and Helen Claire's daughter, Sara, in their small apartment, but as was his wont with anyone who was willing, Gene took them to museums, galleries, and plays. As Helen Claire remembers, "Gene didn't just tell us what he recommended we not miss, but took us himself to the British Museum, the National Gallery, and the Tate. And at each we got the most incredible personal tour, with Gene literally running between the things at each that we just 'couldn't miss,' our own personalized private tour."

Lorraine Bradford gives another example: "When in Russia, I came down with the flu, sick and nervous, so far from home. Gene missed an important event to bring me soup, medicine, and a healing blessing. The blessing told me things that I needed to know. The peace and comfort I felt was indescribable." Karen Rosenbaum, who knew the Englands from their days at Stanford, summarizes, "The hymn 'Because I Have Been Given Much' could be Gene's theme song. He could not see another's lack and not share his and Charlotte's glowing fire, loaf of bread, roof's safe shelter overhead."

## PROVING CONTRARIES

Gene's teaching, writing, and much of his life can be seen through the prism of Joseph Smith's words, "By proving contraries, truth is made manifest." According to Kathryn Shirts, "Eugene England became my model of how to combine deep faith with ethical inquiry. He shared with us his testimony of the gospel and his devotion to the church as well as his concern for social justice, proving to us by his example that they did not have to be at odds."

In a brilliant essay that captures the scope and complexity of England's quest to find harmony between the seemingly contradictory and irreconcilable poles of liberalism and conservatism within Mormonism, Clifton Jolley concludes, "Perhaps the fate of all visionaries is to anticipate more than they can accomplish. And I do not expect to discover whether Gene's efforts to enlarge upon our understanding of our faith—a faith that began on an Upstate New York farm, although its mission and our understanding of it were never intended by God to stay there, whether geographically, theologically, or theocratically—will continue to encourage us to extend ourselves into the future to which Joseph Smith and Gene England instructed us to seek."

## DISCIPLE

For all he accomplished as a teacher, writer, speaker, leader, and activist, we feel the title Gene would like most to be remembered by is disciple of Jesus Christ. Everything Gene did was informed by his complete and consistent devotion to the Savior and his gospel. Gene was a Christian disciple not only in its usual meaning of a follower or devotee, but in its older meaning, *discipere*, "to grasp intellectually, analyze thoroughly," a devotion not only of heart and mind but the two working in concert and harmony.

Gene was fully aware of Josiah Royce's distinction between two kinds of disciples: those Royce refers to as "disciples pure and simple—people who fall under the spell of a person or of a doctrine, and whose whole intellectual life thenceforth consists in their partisanship," and those disciples who are "attracted to a new doctrine by the fact that it gave expression, in a novel way, to some large and deep interest which had already grown up in themselves, and which had already come, more or less independently, to their own consciousness." The disciples of the first sort adhere to "doctrine that has merely to be preached, over and over, in the same terms, [which] cannot possibly be the whole truth." Those of the second sort "are attracted to a new doctrine by the fact that it gave expression, in a novel way, to some large and deep interest which had already grown up in themselves, and which had already come, more or less independently, to their own consciousness."

Royce expands on this distinction between these two kinds of disciples: "Disciples of the first sort often become, as Schopenhauer said, mere magnifying mirrors wherein one sees enlarged all the defects of a doctrine. Disciples of the second sort cooperate in the works of the Spirit; and … help to lead the thought that they accept to a truer expression. They force it beyond its earlier and cruder stages of development," which is exactly what Gene did throughout his life. As his dear friend, Levi Petersen, states, "The quality of Gene's saintliness that I knew most intimately was his profound, instinctive, unyielding belief in the good to be found in human beings. It was a quality I felt simply by being in his presence because I could discern that he was applying it to me … The most important thing about Gene for me was that he made me feel more like a true Mormon. In his presence, I felt my inadequacies diminished and my qualities enhanced." Petersen then expresses a universal sentiment of the contributors to this collection, "God be thanked for the life and influence of Gene England."

# A Note from Charlotte

Some years into our marriage, the story of Gene's birth, as told by his parents, Dora and Eugene, Sr., surfaced. Apparently, the shock on their faces drew the doctor's attention when they observed that Gene's head, with its prominent point, seemed shaped like an upside down ice cream cone! In an attempt to reassure the new parents, the doctor said something about this being a good sign, one of brilliance, a necessary trait for solving problems and staying out of trouble.

I'm sure there is some truth to this story, though which part I can't be certain. It is true that investigating and solving challenging problems and answering difficult questions was part of Gene's nature. This meant, inescapably, that he took risks, if doing so served a good purpose.

His early risk-taking was fairly harmless, like the time he and his best friend, Bert Wilson, played Tarzan in Grandpa England's barn, where they stripped off their shirts and tucked kitchen knives into the waistbands of their shorts. Another time they almost burned the barn down when they innocently started a fire with "just a little hay"! The wheat silo was another tempting place to explore. Rubber guns made of wood, a clothes pin, and a strip of discarded inner tube was all they needed to fire away at each other inside the dark, empty silo. As he grew up, Gene continued to do daring things, only to better purpose.

Leaving the Downy, Idaho farm for Salt Lake City provided a new focus for Gene. He was blessed with some good teachers who helped shape his education. One in particular, Mr. Iverson, an English teacher at East High, nourished Gene's appetite for literature and writing. During this time, along with a group of close friends, Gene discovered the excitement of exploring ideas and asking questions that led to lively discussions, something that continued into college and throughout his life.

Gene was a natural teacher, something he discovered when teaching Samoan children on our mission as newlyweds. He loved teaching, and it soon became clear to him that it would be the focus of his professional life. This was reinforced later at Stanford, where asking questions that challenged traditional answers opened the door to new understandings. It became a hallmark of how Gene learned and taught.

When we returned to Utah after our mission, Gene changed his major from mathematics to English because he loved the way literature presented the human story in all its complexity and evoked the questions he most wanted to explore and grapple with.

Stanford and the people he met there led the way to *Dialogue*, a journal for Latter-day Saints hungry to delve deeply into their faith and its collisions with modern academic, artistic, and religious culture. Given the suspicions of the endeavor among some church leaders, but also seeing the vision of what the journal could accomplish, establishing *Dialogue* was one of the risks he took relative to the church.

As leader of a small branch in Minnesota, where we relocated when Gene accepted a position at St. Olaf's College following his studies at Stanford, Gene continued to think broadly—outside the box—in part by calling church members to lead and teach who seemed unlikely candidates, gradually helping them gain confidence. Being bold and inclusive, Gene considered that all are alike unto God. He believed in the branch members and nurtured them, not from above but while working with them side by side.

Later, in his first year at BYU, Gene, Gary Browning, John Gardner, Bob Bennion, and Suzanne Lundquist explored new and innovative ways for students to learn. The most comprehensive was called colloquium, a class that met several hours a week over the entire academic year. It brought students together from multiple disciplines and the ways they intersected and enriched one another. Fifty years later, that interdisciplinary approach is found in many colleges and universities.

Gene broke trails. He forged ahead. Like the doctor forecast, he solved problems, but he wasn't always successful in staying out of trouble. Most of all, he trusted in the power of love to bless, heal, and bind together those whom he taught, those with whom he worked, and those who were blessed to read his writings. His legacy lives on in the influence he continues to have through his students and colleagues, his writings, and especially through the example he set as a devoted, dedicated Christian disciple.

# "What Are You Willing to Change Your Mind About?" Thinking and Fishing with Gene

**STIRLING ADAMS**

Stirling Adams has lived with his family in Orem, Utah, since 1995, except for year-long family ventures to Argentina, China, Boston, and Europe. While living in those places he missed fishing and hiking the streams and mountains of the Colorado Plateau, while at the same time—perhaps following Gene's lead—he has found good fishing and hiking wherever he's been.

In 1988, for the initial assignment in a BYU class Gene taught on personal essay writing, I wrote a short paper exploring my current experience as a temple missionary. I focused on the pain and dismay I was feeling at the "seemingly secondary eternal roles assigned women in the temple ceremony." From essays written by Gene that I had previously read I had the impression of him as a faithful Mormon and open thinker who was intellectually and spiritually engaged with many of the concepts and events that were most important to me—someone I could and should learn from.

But with the arrogance of a youth with a less than fully developed prefrontal cortex, I also carried the view that Gene had decided in advance that in the case of conflict between his own judgments and those of the church hierarchy, he would take care to err on the side of supporting the status quo. I based this largely on his 1973 *Dialogue* essay, "The Mormon Cross," which concluded with, "The policy of denying Blacks the priesthood [and temple] is rationally untenable from ... historical, theological, ethical, social, psychological, in fact from all perspectives but one: ecclesiastical authority. But for me that perspective outweighs all the others because I am convinced that ecclesiastically the church is doing what the Lord has directed ..."

Because I half-expected Gene to provide justifications that ignored my misgivings with the temple, I hesitated to submit the essay. But I did, and he read it out loud in our next class as an example of the type of writing we would wrestle with during the semester. He returned the essay with a handwritten paragraph of counsel that included the question, "What are you willing to change your mind about?" Then and later, when wrestling with that and other thorny topics, I have tried to push myself to ask that question. In subsequent years, as I paid closer attention to his writing and came to know him as a fly fisher, I recognized that question as a thinking and fishing tool of his own.

Over the next year Gene wrote a couple of articles for the *Student Review*, an "unofficial" weekly magazine produced by students including myself, and for which Gene was an informal advisor. One article was titled "Prior Restraint and Guilt by Association: Reflections on Academic Freedom at BYU." There Gene wrote that he had come to BYU in 1977 with the assumption he would be "[freer] to write and teach what is truly important to me ... than I was at Utah or Stanford or could be at any other university." He reported he had, in fact, "found at BYU that unique freedom to write and teach in ways that combine my faith and my professional training." But, because he had learned BYU had instructed administrators in 1986 not to publish in *Dialogue* or participate in Sunstone conferences, and because of BYU's 1986 decision not to allow *Student Review* to be distributed on campus, he was experiencing a "doubt, small but chilling, whether BYU ... is yet as Christian or as much a real university as our prophets hope for us."

Gene wrote that article several years before the big dust up over academic freedom BYU would undergo in the early 1990s after BYU fired several professors for holding beliefs that were perceived as insufficiently orthodox, leading to years of public debates over the appropriate level of academic freedom for BYU faculty. BYU eventually endured a critical audit from the American Association of University Professionals and developed an academic freedom policy it advertised as balancing institutional interests in orthodoxy against the benefits of academic freedom.

I graduated from BYU in 1989, went to graduate school, and worked elsewhere, then returned to Utah in 1995 to follow my wife's career. After Gene learned I had grown up fishing for trout and salmon on tributaries to the Columbia River in Washington State, he invited me to join him on the Provo River. We fished a few times together—not enough, but enough that when in 1998 a close mutual friend considered joining BYU's Political Science Department, I invited him to join Gene and me fishing.

I told the friend my wife and I would love to have him and his family near us, and he would be great for BYU, but that when he talked with the guys in poli-sci (they were all guys) they would have the same selfish motives as me, and he might hear only about only BYU's positive aspects. I voiced my opinion that BYU had taken a series of unfortunate turns, and as a breaking example, at that very time BYU was working to push Gene out. I opined that the larger issue was that just as some financial institutions have claimed since the 1970s that they are "too big to fail," we Mormons have a set of theological beliefs that some believe are "too wrong to fail," or "too tragic and enormous to be corrected," because correcting these beliefs I suggested could lead members to doubt other church beliefs or practices. Prominent examples of these beliefs were the church's former exclusion of people with Black African ancestry from priesthood ordination and the temple endowment, and our continuing acceptance of the theology behind polygamy.

Gene had written prominently about both of those issues. I argued to my friend that while Gene might be seen in a different culture as a safe company man because, in the end he argued that God approved the church's practices, he had been identified by the too-wrong-to-fail crowd as a serious threat because he didn't reach his safe conclusions until after daring to analyze and sometimes criticizing justifications proffered for questionable practices. In his writing he asked himself and the church the potentially dangerous question, "What are you willing to change your mind about?" and he was punished for doing so. "Come fishing with us," I said to my friend, and hear a more complete story about what it's like to work and think at BYU.

So, one morning before dawn, we three gathered at Gene's home and drove two hours south, up Fairview Canyon and along Skyline Drive, which runs a hundred miles over the mountains forming the Wasatch Plateau. At ten thousand feet, it overlooks to the west the small towns of the Sanpete Valley; to the east lie the Book Cliffs. We parked at one of the subalpine lakes near a summit and hiked down two thousand feet in elevation. Then we fished up a stream in return.

On our drive, and during our hike across meadows of rice grass and down steep and steeper slopes, we covered obligatory themes Mormon men of a certain age and rural Pacific Northwest background discuss while fishing: sex, religion, politics, environmental policy, and more sex and religion.

The stream water ran low, and the trout were skittish. But, if we used a fine tippet, carefully crept up on a pool or riffle, and cast without throwing a shadow, there was success to be had. At one point, I climbed out of a valley to leave a stretch of stream to Gene. After reaching the horizon, I sat and watched him fish far below. He crouched and carefully walked toward a pool formed by a beaver dam. He cast for a few minutes with one fly, then another, without success. He moved to the next hole, also formed by beaver. This time Gene dropped to his hands and knees and wriggled slowly forward, almost prone, like the Idaho farm boy he once was, sliding under barb wire. He caught two trout from that pool. As he brought in the second, I realized I had just observed someone asking and answering: "What are you willing to change your mind about?"

In the late afternoon, as we crossed a marshy meadow heading home, I initiated the conversation. Academic freedom was waning at BYU. Some of BYU's best professors were being forced out. I speculated that with recent stands the church had taken on same-sex marriage in Hawaii and Alaska, a new front was coming for tension withing the church over scholarship and things could get worse. Did Gene think BYU was a place where our friend would and should flourish?

The short version of the ensuing conversation is that Gene told us how BYU was the very best place in the world for him because there he was allowed to seriously bring the gospel into his classes, and to conduct research like he could nowhere else. Gene said he thought our friend was likely to have the same positive experience. I was flabbergasted. I remember thinking, "But Gene, they won't let you teach in the honors program or teach religion classes anymore! They are forcing you out—they are punishing you for your research and writing!"

Less than a year later, after BYU asked Gene to resign, he moved to Utah Valley State College and started a religious studies program. At a public lecture there, I heard Gene tell an audience he was at the place where he could most seriously bring the gospel into his classes, and where he could perform research like nowhere else. On hearing that, my first thought was that Gene was cast in the mold of Voltaire's Dr. Pangloss—given to regarding the world, however it was, as necessarily the best of all possible worlds. I've since come to think instead it may be that Gene was better at the long game than me, perhaps because he was a better historian, and humbler and wiser. Also, maybe he was better at asking, "What are you willing to change your mind about?"

# Remembering Gene

## LAVINA FIELDING ANDERSON

Lavina Fielding Anderson, president of Editing, Inc., was former copy editor and editor of the *Journal of Mormon History* and the *Association for Mormon Letters Annual*. She was also copy editor of *Dialogue: A Journal of Mormon Thought* and *The Review of Higher Education*. With Gene England, she coedited *Tending the Garden: Essays on Mormon Literature*. She was the editor of *Lucy's Book: A Critical Edition of Lucy Mack Smith's Family Memoir* and, prior to her death in 2023, was working on *Lucy's Life: A Biography of Lucy Mack Smith* (forthcoming, Signature Books). Her essays about a tumultuous life in the church were published in *Mercy without End: Toward a More Inclusive Church* (Signature Books, 2020).

I was a member of the *Ensign* staff, one of several college graduates that managing editor Jay Todd had mobilized to move the staid *Improvement Era* in a more contemporary direction. My roommate, Jill Mulvay, was working for Church Historian Leonard Arrington and drew me into association with the fine young historians that formed the division. My flourishing interest in Mormon women's history appealed to Jay as a productive area for future articles, and he gave me the challenging assignment of Mormon history and Mormon women. I eagerly accepted.

Just across the hall from Leonard's division was Florence S. Jacobsen, former president of the Young Women's Mutual Improvement Association, preserver and restorer of the Lion House, and granddaughter of two church presidents: Joseph F. Smith and Heber J. Grant. My husband, Paul, was fresh from earning his master's in architecture from Princeton University and was a recipient of one of Leonard's summer fellowships, which he applied to surveying Mormon architecture, especially its chapels, stake centers, and temples. Florence and Paul saw eye to eye on the horrendous destruction of Mormon historic architecture conducted by the Church Building Department. Florence quickly offered Paul a position as her architectural expert. He would expand those duties into helping to design the Museum of Church History and Art and later the Museum of Art at BYU.

I was passionately devoted to *Dialogue*, thanks to the first issue that I read on my mission in France. Jay Todd saw in its openness and quality a direction church magazines could profit from. I was delighted to discover that Gene was working part time for Leonard, researching and writing on Brigham Young.

Gene submitted an article to the *Ensign* that would be published under the title of "Speaking the Truth in Love" (April 1976). In it, Gene made three suggestions for achieving that goal: sincerity, moral courage, and a vulnerable sharing of spiritual experiences. Each point was illustrated with stories from Mormon history, Gene's personal and family experiences, and especially the scriptures.

I was negotiating some recommended revisions with Gene. In one example of speaking the truth without love, he had given a sacrament meeting talk on the law of consecration that a speaker at the next testimony meeting rebutted point by point. Hurt and angry, Gene struggled with his feelings; but, after sincere prayer, he made an appointment with this brother, apologized for offending him, and asked forgiveness. The other man accepted that apology, expressed forgiveness, and in turn apologized for his attack on Gene. Though they held and recognized continued differences, they became friends.

It was clear to me that the zealousness in Gene's article would re-offend not only this brother but many other church members by hinting at what could be interpreted as a claim to moral superiority. Gene willingly agreed to rewrite the experience. In fact, Gene apologized to me, admitting that he had no doubt offended me as well. I agreed that it was not what I had expected from the author of "That They Might Not Suffer: The Gift of the Atonement," which asserted that, rather than seeing the Atonement as a ransom or debt repayment, the power of the Savior's Atonement lay in the transformation of his love in inspiring us to repent.

This doctrinal discussion led to a deeper conversation about Gene's efforts to understand and live by gospel principles. I asked him why he was not teaching at the Institute full time or, better yet, at BYU. He candidly said he had been rejected for a faculty position at BYU. I was startled and asked, "But why?" He smiled and said, "It seems that I was too Mormon for St. Olaf's"—the Lutheran college in Minnesota where he had previously taught—"and I'm not Mormon enough for BYU." As other episodes would show, even after Gene was hired by BYU's English Department, where he taught for twenty-one years, this paradox would remain alive.

I loved the article and was proud that the *Ensign* published it, although I recall coming out of my office at one point and exclaiming, "I've got to disable Gene England's italics key!" His desire to emphasize the important points in his text with this typographical function did, I'll admit, go far toward replicating the rhythms and intonation of his speech. As a postscript, even after Gene's rewriting satisfied the *Ensign* staff, I asked him for another revision, since the Adult Correlation Committee, which reviewed all the *Ensign*'s articles, seemed to take real pleasure in pouncing on so-called doctrinal errors. Gene patiently complied, even though he felt that some of the requested changes blurred the challenge captured in the title. Gene wrote other articles for church magazines, and dealing with the Correlation Committee did not become easier, but he remained patient.

* * *

Paul had been a Stanford undergraduate and a student in one of Gene's Institute classes, and Gene observed our friendship-turning-into-courtship with interest and approval. He was also a fine example of not meddling or matchmaking. When we became engaged, he asked either Paul or me—or maybe both of us when we were together—what our plans were for a honeymoon locale. We didn't have one at that point, and he offered us the cabin he and Charlotte had recently finished. We gratefully accepted and, a few days before the wedding, Gene gave us the keys, a map to the cabin, instructions on how to turn on the water heater, and a quick overview of the cooking equipment. We had a week to enjoy the peace and solitude of the cabin, which had large windows and, architecturally, a message about Gene and Charlotte's generosity. Its broad wrap-around padded window seats were an invitation to gather for firesides or informal discussions, followed by sleepovers. Paul and I were looking for privacy. Gene and Charlotte were looking for opportunities to share. It was a loving message to think about as we began our marriage.

* * *

Later, as another part of my *Ensign* assignment when Gene was teaching at BYU, I called him and said, "I'd like to come down and talk about some article ideas." He enthusiastically agreed; and a few days later, I drove to Provo and found him wedged in his office surrounded by piles of books, papers, and other academic impedimenta. There was not room to sit and have a discussion, and someone else was already propped against the door. We walked across the quad to the Cougareat where I went off to collect my lunch while Gene said, "I'll hold this table." When I carried my tray back, I expected Gene to make his lunchtime selections. He pulled out a Red Delicious apple and, seeing my raised eyebrows, said, "Yes, the food here is a good buy, but having apples for lunch this week means I can add ten dollars to our fast offering." I forget the article ideas we talked about, but I'll never forget the lesson.

* * *

Gene became concerned about how to implement President Kimball's address on "Miltons and Shakespeares of Our Own," an expansive encouragement to Mormon writers and artists that had aroused much enthusiasm. Since Elder Boyd K. Packer's "The Arts and the Spirit of the Lord" had thrown a large bucket of ice water on any form of creativity that did not explicitly support conservative Mormon values, there was considerable confusion on the topic. A prominent theme in discussions, as a result, was the role that insightful, encouraging, and mature criticism could play.

In this context, I got a call from Maureen Ursenbach Beecher in Leonard's history division inviting me to a gathering with Gene and Steven P. Sondrup, both of whom were then teaching at BYU, to discuss how to foster helpful criticism. I think Levi Peterson and Condadai Seshachari from Weber State University were also present. Maureen hosted the meeting in a small conference room in the LDS Church Historical Department. Although we had convened at Gene's suggestion, he sat back listening, letting the group explore the topic. We all agreed that insightful and professional criticism would greatly advance Mormon literature. Maureen suggested the name: not "The Association *of* Mormon Literature" but "The Association *for* Mormon Literature."

After about an hour, Gene glanced at his watch, leaned forward to put his elbows on the table, and said, "Maureen, why don't you chair an executive meeting that will spell out the purposes of good criticism, find a date for an organizational meeting, and oversee the election of officers?" Then he was gone, leaving us rather breathless. Everyone at the meeting eventually became president of the association. Steven served loyally and efficiently as executive secretary until his retirement from BYU. AML is still thriving to this day.

* * *

I once asked Gene how he could bear so gracefully the burden of being a role model to so many. It was telling that he shrugged off the idea of being a "liberal icon or role model," but instead said that what he wanted to be "for so many" was a servant, following in the footsteps of the Savior. Focusing on "how to serve rather than how I am perceived" made impossible things possible. One of those impossible things was enduring the brutal treatment and misunderstandings that surrounded him, first because of his association with *Dialogue* and second because he always thought, spoke, and acted from his understanding of core gospel principles. Why did he frighten so many figures who held power in the church?

* * *

When I move beyond the veil, I will continue unfinished conversations with a long list of people. A realization that helps me anticipate that time with rejoicing is that my dialogue with Gene will continue.

# The Three Times I Met Gene England

**MICHAEL AUSTIN**

Michael Austin is the provost and vice president of academic affairs at Snow College in Ephraim, Utah. He is the author or editor of fifteen books, including *Rereading Job*, *Vardis Fisher: A Mormon Novelist*, and *The Testimony of Two Nations: How the Book of Mormon Reads and Rereads the Bible*. In 2022, he was awarded the Lifetime Achievement Award from the Association for Mormon Letters.

## I

The first time I met Gene, I was a graduate student in BYU's Department of English. Let's call it 1991; though, really, it could have been any time between fall of 1990 and spring of 1992. I am fuzzy about the date, but I have vivid memories of the meeting itself. I was a teaching assistant for one of the large British literature survey classes at BYU—a position that, under certain circumstances (and only when accompanied by a professor), permitted me to enter the faculty lounge on the second floor of the old JKHB. At the end of one semester, all the TAs for the various large classes were in the lounge with their professors working on final grades. My group was busily calculating paper and exam grades, adding participation points, and deducting points for unexcused absences—more accounting than teaching, but it had to be done. Right next to us, Gene was leading his TAs in prayer.

This was not a general "please help us be sensitive to our students' needs" kind of prayer. They were going through the class list in alphabetical order, and Gene was asking God for specific inspiration about every student in a class of more than two hundred people. Even at BYU, even in the 1990s, this was strange behavior. Nobody else that I knew prayed about grades. A few professors occasionally opened a class session with a prayer, and everyone made a good-faith effort to mention how Wordsworth's "trailing clouds of glory" and Blake's "fearful symmetry" might approximate gospel principles if we squint at them just right. But this was different. Gene was not posturing for the administration or playing to a crowd. He really wanted to know what God thought about his students' grades, and he fully expected to get answers.

I had never met Gene before that day, but I knew who he was. I read (and loved) *Dialogues with Myself* before my mission, when I was a freshman accounting major. I knew that he had clashed with the religion department and that he had been rebuked by Apostle Bruce R. McConkie (though not by name) in his infamous "Seven Deadly Heresies" talk—which I owned and listened to multiple times on my mission. But I left the faculty lounge that day with a certain knowledge that Eugene England was no heretic; he was Mormon to his core. And not just culturally. Gene believed in the church, its scriptures, and its leaders with the same sincerity that he believed in the value of open-minded inquiry, dialogue, and the power of communities to come together to discover and shape their truths. These were not conflicting loyalties for Gene, nor were they non-overlapping magisteria. They were two completely non-severable elements of his religion.

## II

The next time I met Gene was in August of 1991, when we both ended up on the same panel at a Sunstone Symposium. The symposium occurred just as the United States began its military buildup in the Persian Gulf, in preparation for what would become the First Gulf War, and our panel was on the moral necessity of pacifism. Both of our talks had been part of a larger panel that was split into two sessions to give speakers more time to talk. Gene and I were the only presenters in our session, so we both got to speak for about half an hour. I gave what I considered at the time to be a logical, organized, and impassioned plea for the United States to exercise military restraint because that is what Christ would have us do. It was a timely and straightforward argument that, I can now see, was just the sort of shallow, jingoistic manifesto preferred by graduate students with more sensibility than sense. All I was saying was "give peace a chance."

Gene, on the other hand, read a story about going fly fishing. This was an early version of his essay, "Monte Cristo," later published in his book, *Making Peace*. At the time, I thought that the story was at once prosaic and disturbing. In paragraph after paragraph of thick description, Gene described how his friend, Frank, taught him to tie flies, cast with his wrist, and find the best spots in the river to catch trout. I still remember being slightly disturbed by Gene's long description of killing and gutting two of the trout to cook on a campfire—and by a conversation he reported about another friend's daughter being stabbed to death by her football-player boyfriend when she tried to break up with him. I kept waiting for him to bring the story back around to peace, or the Gulf War, or the morality of killing fish as long as you eat them with butter—or to draw some conclusion from his experience relevant to the topic of the panel. But other than the intriguing detail that he accidentally left his knife on the riverbank when they hiked out, nothing in the story seemed to have much to do with peace.

This too, I later discovered, was classic Gene. He drew few distinctions between writing scholarship, making political arguments, and simply telling stories about his life. Because he didn't separate his life into these compartments, it simply didn't occur to him that his scholarship might not reflect his religion or that his personal experiences would not express his political and religious beliefs. Gene integrated these aspects of himself more effectively and completely than any human being I have ever known. And he expected everyone else to recognize, and even replicate, the fundamental coherence of his personality. Of course, he would expect us to understand the political and spiritual implications of a day spent fly fishing in the Monte Cristo Mountains. Why should he destroy the beautiful, nuanced coherence of his life by turning profound experiences into bumper stickers? I still struggle to live with the kind of non-compartmentalized integrity that Gene demonstrated in his life's work.

### III

The last time I met Gene was in January of 2001. He had retired from BYU, not by choice, and taken a position as a writer-in-residence at Utah Valley State College (now Utah Valley University). I was teaching at Shepherd College, a public school in West Virginia, where I had recently become chair of the English Department. I approached Gene by email and asked him to write a letter to my tenure and promotion committee contextualizing several articles about Mormon literature that I had published in *Dialogue* while I was in graduate school. I needed his help convincing my colleagues that these were actual academic articles read by real professors and not just weird Mormon stuff that nobody noticed. Gene wrote a wonderful letter for me, and we continued corresponding.

At some point in the correspondence, Gene told me that he had received an NEH grant to study the feasibility of Mormon studies programs at public universities. I told him that my university hosted an Appalachian heritage festival every year and suggested that he look at how other universities had incorporated Appalachian and other regional studies programs into their humanities curricula. Gene agreed, and he invited me to Provo to give a talk about how regional cultural studies programs might serve as models for Mormon Studies at UVSC.

After my talk, Gene invited me to his home, and we stayed up most of the night talking about Mormon studies. He suggested that I apply for an open position at UVSC and see if I could become part of the English Department there; then he and I could work together on a large NEH grant to start a full-scale Mormon studies center. In much the same way that Gene spent his time at BYU trying to convince Mormons to take academic work seriously, he planned to spend his time at UVSC trying to convince academics to take Mormonism seriously.

Gene's vision thrilled me, and I wanted to be a part of it. We had to cut the discussion short, however, when Gene began experiencing a migraine headache of the sort that had been plaguing him throughout my visit. I left Provo on January 18, 2001, excited by Gene's plans but concerned for his health. One month later I learned that doctors had discovered a massive tumor in his brain. Despite a successful surgery and promising results with initial treatment, Gene died on August 19, 2001.

Although I only met Gene three times, each of my interactions with him changed the way that I saw myself and the world. Gene convinced me that there were vibrant and vital things within Mormonism that I still needed to find and tell the world about—and that the world would listen if I told the stories well enough. At great expense to himself, Gene hacked away at biases and pre-conceptions in both academia and Mormonism to create the spaces where I and many others continue to stand. We have a place to live because Gene cleared the ground.

# I Was Blessed to Have Known Him

**ROBIN ZENGER BAKER**

Robin Zenger Baker is currently a family therapist practicing in the Boston area. She has taught organizational behavior at Boston University, been an office manager for Glance Networks, served as president of *Exponent II*, and written a book about adult children making choices that are difficult for parents. She has enjoyed strong relationships with all of the England family over the years and recognizes that her childhood was infinitely more fun and adventurous because of them.

Gene England was playful, fun, a little impulsive, and a man with a vision. He was also my best friend's father, which put him squarely on the sidelines of the relevant domain of my childhood. But his impact on me grew over the years.

Growing up in Palo Alto, there were five families in our church community who gathered for play, holidays, and competitions: Zengers, Englands, Christensens, Taylors, and Finlaysons. Each family had between five and eight children who were approximately the same ages. I became especially close to the Englands, partly because their family had five girls and one boy, while mine had the opposite ratio of five boys and one girl (me), thus making them an ideal retreat from my boy-centered world.

Some joint family adventures included picnicking on Sunday afternoons at Foothill Park and kayaking, eating Kentucky Fried Chicken, and evening runs for ice cream to the local Baskin-Robbins and Edy's. We played Capture the Flag at Rinconada Park in the dark, held family Olympics, vacationed along the foggy Santa Cruz coastline, and cracked the walls of the Taylors' home hitting piñatas to celebrate the New Year. We also got countless cases of poison oak at our jointly owned Bearmont, a redwood-filled retreat off Skyline Boulevard which Gene had talked several families into purchasing. Bearmont was where we often retreated on weekends to connect with nature and friends, camp in a rustic setting without bathrooms, showers, or even running water, explore, find salamanders, and build campfires.

One favorite memory was of all the kids piling on top of the station wagons as soon as we entered the skinny, rutted dirt road, holding on to the luggage racks to enjoy the scenery and the thrill of breaking all reasonable child-rearing rules. We also loved the excitement of riding in the Englands' car, because when Gene was driving, he was liable to hit the gas just as we approached an incline so the car would catch air. (This tendency to drive past his vision may have led to Charlotte's eventual insistence on doing the driving herself more often.) I knew even as a kid that this adventurous life at Bearmont would never have happened without the influence of Gene England; and these adventures mostly ended when the Englands eventually moved to Minnesota when Gene began his work at St. Olaf's College.

As I grew up, Gene's influence on me increased. I came of age knowing that the church was imperfect, but nevertheless wonderful and necessary for my soul, partly because of Gene's article, "Why the Church is as True as the Gospel." I grew up in an atmosphere of being willing to question, partly because Gene was so vocal about his views that Blacks needed the priesthood. Referring to Gene's willingness to value honest questioning, some commented that Gene liked to "poke a bear with a stick" when he got under the skin of various church authorities. But I admired how Gene was such a man of action—starting Food for Poland where he saw the need and speaking his mind in such forthright ways. People close to me with struggling faith sought him out to bolster their faith, and I never wondered about his commitment to the church.

One year my husband, Rich, and I visited Gene and Charlotte while they were leading a study abroad group in London. Gene took us at a fast pace through the streets of London, chasing the best plays and most exciting art. During downtimes, he patiently explained the ins and outs of the game of cricket to Rich, thrilled to have another man with whom to share his love of sports.

On another occasion, Gene and Charlotte came to Boston so Gene could speak at a student event in Cambridge. We picked Gene up at the Longfellow Park chapel afterward, where he was sitting on the steps with a pencil sticking out of his ear, a habit Charlotte worried about, but she understood because, as she said, his ears always seemed to be itchy. During this visit, we decided to watch the Boston Marathon and, since Gene was Gene, we ended up at the finish line with the hordes. When our small son, Scott, got frustrated at being unable to see much, Gene plopped him up on his shoulders.

Our last visit with Gene was after he was diagnosed with brain tumors and was in a wheelchair. He came to my mother's wedding in the Little America Hotel in Salt Lake City, lovingly attended by Charlotte and several of his daughters. Even though this was shortly before his passing and speaking was difficult for him, Gene wanted to be there to express his love for my mother and his happiness for her happiness.

I stood in awe of Gene. I feel blessed to have known him as my good friend Katherine's father, my friend Charlotte's husband, the guy who put my son on his shoulders to see the marathon better, the guy who shared the details of cricket with my husband, and the man who helped my family members stay close to the church. My direct conversations with Gene may have been few, but he made a huge difference in my life. His example, his writing, his influence on my family and others in my life has made my life richer and my understanding of what matters clearer. I feel keenly what a blessing it was to have known him.

# Gene (and Charlotte) Remembered (from Afar)

**CONNIE BENNION**

The daughter of a professor and university president, Constance "Connie" Wilson Bennion spent most of her childhood living in and around college campuses, which fostered her lifelong love of learning. She graduated summa cum laude from the University of Oregon and did graduate work at the University of Minnesota in English and history. Connie and her husband, David, reared their six children in Palo Alto, California, and were mission leaders in Geneva, Switzerland. Connie resides in Pleasant Grove, Utah, and loves being grandmother to twenty-two.

It was a long time ago and I no longer remember all of the details. What I do remember is that it was one of those small periods of time that has made all the difference in my life. Gene and Charlotte are pivotal to my life's story.

After doing some graduate work at the University of Minnesota in 1965–66, I signed a contract to teach English and history to eighth- and ninth-graders in San Jose, California. I had been invited to share an apartment in Sunnyvale with longtime friends, Margot Noall and Janet Lindstrom, and a cousin, Ann Jacobs. I was stepping into a new chapter of life in more ways than I recognized.

One night I was home alone when the doorbell rang. When I opened the door, I saw Larry Brim, a Stanford graduate student and our apartment manager, standing outside.

"Excuse me," he said. "I want to begin by saying I am a happily married man and will not come into your apartment, but I was home studying for a test and had a strong feeling I needed to come and knock on your door and get better acquainted. Where are you from?"

"St. Paul, Minnesota."

"What were you doing there?"

"Going to graduate school."

"At the University of Minnesota?"

"Yes."

"Well, that is where Meredith Wilson is president, isn't it?"

"Yes."

"Do you know anything about him?"

"I certainly do. He is my father."

"Your father! Well, he is a Mormon, isn't he?"

"Yes, he is."

"Then you must be a Mormon too."

"Yes, I am, but I don't know as much about the church as I wish I did. I was hoping to get better acquainted with it, but I am doing a terrible job of it. I don't even know the way to the church."

"Well, I am the elders quorum president, and I will have a ride for you Sunday morning at 9:30."

The ride was provided as promised. I sat in the back row of the chapel and was filled with a strong mix of feelings. I couldn't begin to understand what was going on and doubted if I would return.

During the closing song, a member of the bishopric got up out of his chair on the stand and came and sat beside me. Following the closing prayer, he introduced himself as Eugene England, asked me a few questions, and invited me to his family's home for dinner. He assured me I would love his wife. He said he and Charlotte had six wonderful but noisy children and that there was a "fireside" planned for his home that evening for which I could stay and meet some wonderful ward members.

And so …

That is one of the moments when my life took a new direction and became filled with new meaning. This first meeting of the Englands marked the beginning of a lifelong friendship with Gene and Charlotte. For me, Gene's name has become synonymous with "teacher." The gifts he has added to my mind, heart, and spirit are too large to be measured and too meaningful to imagine living without.

I would have loved Charlotte wherever and whenever I might have met her, but at this time and in this context I had ample opportunity to become acquainted not only with her unique personality, natural charm, and personal warmth, but also her deep spirituality, all of which has been a treasure to me since that very first day.

Gene and Charlotte are two of my angels as well as two of my favorite friends. Without them I would not have married my husband, David, nor been blessed with our six children and twenty-two grandchildren. I shudder at the very thought; I love them both more than words can tell, or tapes can measure.

# Experiencing Gene England

**JOHN BENNION**

John Bennion has published a collection of short fiction and six novels: *Falling Toward Heaven* (Signature Books, 2000), *An Unarmed Woman* (Signature Books, 2019), *Ezekiel's Third Wife* (Roundfire Books, 2019), *Spin* (BCC Press, 2022), *Ruth at the End of the Earth* (BCC Press, 2023), and *Antelope Spring* (BCC Press, 2025). He has published short stories and essays in a number of journals and magazines, including *Southwest Review*, *Dialogue*, *Literature and Belief*, *BYU Studies*, *Sunstone*, and others. He has retired from teaching creative writing in the English Department at Brigham Young University.

Gene was one of the first professors to welcome me when I interviewed and then was hired by the English Department at Brigham Young University. He helped influence the department to accept my application. During my first year, I shadowed him in his Mormon literature class where his practice was to invite writers to visit and talk to the students about their careers. He arranged for students and faculty to meet with such writers as Walter Kern, Levi Peterson, Maurine Whipple, and many others important to Mormon literature. In fact, his course was the inspiration for the English Department Reading Series, which has since grown to include writers of national and international fame. Gene knew that his job as a teacher, especially on the study abroad courses he led, was to give students experiences through conversing with writers, attending and discussing plays, and engaging in service projects. His paradigm was learning by doing and then thinking, talking, and writing about doing.

Gene influenced me not only as a teacher of Mormon literature, but as an experiential educator who valued reflection on action. His continual acts of reflection on himself, literature, and the practice of the gospel made him a pioneer and a mapmaker who enabled others to chart their own course. His analysis of Mormon letters in "The Dawning of a Brighter Day" is a map that was never intended to be a resolution of the issues, but rather an invitation to others to explore. That has proved to be the case. I and numerous others have extended the discussion on the past, present, and future of Mormon Letters.

From what he did, not only what he said, I knew Gene cared about his students and also his fellow teachers. His office was a mess. I don't think that one word can communicate the chaos, the stacks of papers and books that covered his desk, part of the floor, and his bookshelves. I've heard it said that one can tell the state of someone's mind by the state of his or her office, and his mind was a hive of both spontaneous and planned connections. Gene was a wildly creative teacher. He prepared, but his flight plan would have made most other teachers feel that they were just wandering. I loved this capriciousness in his teaching, talking, and writing. He bucked convention so well because he was not afraid of being himself. His selective regard for convention grew out of his formidable conscience but also out of his concern for those who would be most harmed by the conventions imposed by powerful people. He mapped the terrain of the soul, and he did it by building bridges to many kinds of people. One example is that during the 1990s, when the department was suffering our own version of the Troubles, Gene cleaned his office—a herculean effort. Then he sent out an email inviting anyone to come and break homemade bread with him. He had butter and honey as well. I don't know if his actions alone helped heal the department. Healing was accomplished by time and the gradual breaking down of what had seemed permanent divisions. But his good heart was a stable force in the department and in my life. His heart, which he searched perpetually, is exemplified in "Easter Weekend." This essay moves me every time I read it, especially the last line, "I'm sorry in all the world."

His wry humor was famous, or possibly infamous to those who didn't understand him. He accepted my story "Dust" in his fiction collection *Bright Angels and Familiars*. He often referred to the story as "Dirt," and then laughed like hell. At the time, I thought he was chiding me for the sexual content, but more recently I have wondered if he wasn't referring to the importance of the place, the desert landscape, in the story. His teasing then might be because I was a desert farm boy. He grew up in Downey, a superior location for farming because it receives seventeen inches of rain instead of the ten falling on my home landscape.

For years, we were in the same writing group. Charlotte is still in that group. I've been in their home many times before and after his death. Much of the house is built of found material, bricks or wood from other homes. This is emblematic of the Englands' inclusive nature, a drawing together of many elements. The home they created is full of people, some who needed a place to live and some visiting for an hour or an evening. The walls are consciously permeable. When I think of Gene, he leans back in his chair, smiling with his mouth and his eyes from below his thick, sandy brows. "Welcome," he seems to say. "Tell me what you're thinking and I'll do the same, and we'll see how deep we can go."

# He Altered the Course of My Religious Life

**MOLLY MCLELLAN BENNION**

Molly McLellan Bennion, retired attorney of Seattle, Washington, has served on the board of the Dialogue Foundation since its inception three decades ago. She loves teaching her granddaughter's youth Sunday school class and introducing a new generation to Gene.

Had there been no Eugene England, there would probably have been no LDS membership for me. I joined the church the year after Gene and his terrific colleagues founded *Dialogue, A Journal of Mormon Thought*. Though I began considering the church when I dated a Mormon in 1962, I resisted joining until I found *Dialogue* one afternoon as I sat on the dusty floor of the religion section of Harvard's Widener Library. (I also found copies of the original *Exponent*, another but less important piece in my conversion puzzle.) That same high school date, now my husband, convinced his advisor to issue me a Widener pass to use whenever I visited from Smith College. I devoured that first year of *Dialogue*. In its pages I found a home, a home I had not found in five years of personal study and frequent church attendance. So many church doctrines resonated with me, but some didn't. The male-centric culture didn't. The racist culture didn't. The unquestioning culture didn't.

Gene wrote in the first issue of "doubt as a condition that can be productive if it leads one to seek and knock and ask …" Yes! He taught, "We must truly listen to each other, respecting our essential brotherhood …" and that "dialogue can serve both truth and charity." Yes! A Lutheran, I wrestled with mainstream Mormon dismissal of grace until Gene published Lowell Bennion's excellent sermon, "For By Grace Are Ye Saved" in Volume 1, Number 4. Yes! He featured nonmembers, questioning historians, probing theologians, people of thoughtful faith and the doubt which must be its companion. YES! If there was room in the church for people like Gene, I would try to see if there was a place for me too.

Decades later, Gene and a handful of devoted *Dialogue* editors, writers, and one consumer (me) formed the journal's first governing board. Heretofore, *Dialogue*'s editors and editorial boards had performed all the functions necessary to produce the journal, but volunteer labor was getting hard to find. The *Dialogue* board took over the business functions to free the editors and editorial boards to create the journal itself. It worked beautifully and remains a better model.

But, of course, human as they are, boards are not trouble-free models. I had met some of the board but knew none of them well. At my first meeting, I quickly sensed tension between a few members, all fine people. It was more personality than philosophy. We were all devoted to the same cause, Gene's cause. Unfortunately, some conflicts predated the board. In addition, speaking styles ranged from abrupt to reticent. We weren't always communicating on the same wavelength. Gene was not with us long, but while he was, he was the peacemaker. He read the tensions and intervened with great love and skill to ease troubled feelings and keep us working together productively. He did it seamlessly, never silencing, always inviting lovingly. When he became too sick to continue, others had to fill his shoes. With Gene's example, they largely did. Gene deserves much credit for the second and current organizational phase of his journal.

Gene was a seeker and a teacher who taught others to seek. I am just one of many who remember brief moments with Gene the teacher. Once, as he and Charlotte drove me to the airport, he asked if I had read a new Mormon fiction writer. I said I had started the novel but dropped it. It was dark and crude. Gene gently chastised me for failing to see it through to what he found to be stunning beauty. He went on to talk of that beauty and the need to be more open to possibilities. I don't remember the title or the author, but I remember his lesson. A small moment at the feet of a teacher endures beside the big moments that altered the course of my religious life.

# Gene, the Generous Genius

## SCOTT BRADFORD

Scott Bradford grew up in Arlington, Virginia, with excellent parents, Charles and Mary, and superb older siblings, Steve and Lorraine. He married his luminescent wife, Sharon Aldous, in 1989, and they have five children, four children-in-law, and, at this writing, five grandchildren. A faculty member of the BYU Economics Department, Scott conducts research in international economics and helps bright young adults along their chosen paths. Outside of work and family, Scott enjoys serving in the church, as well as museums, nature (terrestrial and celestial), performing arts, reading, sightseeing, and sports (often lazily watching them, sometimes actually participating in them).

Sharon and I piled into the car with my mother, Mary Lythgoe Bradford, and Gene and Charlotte. (For as long as I can remember, I have called them simply Gene and Charlotte, never Brother and Sister England, even though they are my social superiors and deserve more esteem than first names usually convey. In their case, though, "Gene" and "Charlotte" stem from a sincere affectionate respect.) We were going to dinner at the Grille at Sundance. Sharon and I had recently moved to Provo, and my mom was visiting from Virginia. Sharon and I both felt genuinely honored to be included in a night out with my mother and her decades-long friends. We also looked forward to eating at a nice restaurant, since such chances came only sporadically to new professor families like us.

The Grille resembles Gene and Charlotte's home: lots of wood and earth tones, an open door, great willingness to serve you top-notch food and make you comfortable. Those two places, though, do differ in one crucial way: the Grille expects payment; Gene and Charlotte never have.

We had a great time. My weak memory does not allow me to recall what the conversation covered. (Strangely, this same memory *can* recall the entire starting line-up of the 1977 Pittsburgh Pirates.) At the end of the meal, Mary ended up paying. She usually does. With pen in hand, she pondered the tip. I stood ready to help with the calculation, as I often had in the past.

At this moment, Gene made a curious statement. "Be generous, Mary," he said. Now, I, at least, would not expect such advice in that situation. Often, one of the older men, such as Gene, pays the bill. In addition, one rarely hears one who is not paying give unsolicited tip advice to the payer. So, Gene's counsel struck me as singular. Further, Grille servers earn good wages. Why even be generous with someone who really doesn't need it?

Despite my briefly raised eyebrows, his statement did not offend us at all because it was pure Gene, the Gene that we love so much. So, while Miss Manners may have frowned upon what he said, each of us knew that he had done nothing improper. In fact, I do not think that any of us outwardly acknowledged what he said. I discussed it with Mary and Sharon after the fact but never at length. I write of it now because that incident evokes much of Gene's goodness.

Gene had a gift. He could, without hypocrisy, encourage the rest of us to share without he himself literally leading by example. Thus, Gene could say, "Be generous, Mary," and have that be exactly the right thing for him to say, even though he was not paying. He led by example of a different sort. Instead of literally leading the way with monetary giving, he lived a life of generosity and charity manifest in a myriad of other ways, many of them ingenious. He did share material things, but, more than that, he shared his charity-loving self. Like his home, he left his heart unlocked, freely and openly sharing its contents and always welcoming the chance to connect with others.

## CLASSROOM

As a professor, Gene shared his passion for literature, his love for its power to teach us and inspire us to live beautifully, its ability to warn us away from the ugly. I got a full dose of this in the "Learning How to Learn" Colloquium, during the 1981–1982 year at BYU. This was a multidisciplinary six-hour full-year course taught by five faculty members: Gene, Robert Bennion (psychology), John Gardner (physics), Suzanne Lundquist (English), and Sue Peterson (English). I learned much from each of those professors. We read and wrestled with *The Brothers Karamazov*, *Hamlet*, *King Lear*, and the Book of Job; learned calculus and then taught it to our hapless roommates; dug into the mind-boggling implications of quantum mechanics; took on *The Trickster*; and explored geology and evolution. Along with the other professors, Gene taught us of the integrity/charity triangle, which has self, others, and God at each vertex. He helped us to see that we must act with integrity toward each point of the triangle and that one can only do so by cultivating charity (or *agape*).

The core theme that enabled him to pull all of this together was the Atonement. I think that the main reason that Gene loved Dostoyevsky and Shakespeare is that their works enabled him to teach the Atonement. Clifton Fadiman said, "To read Dostoyevsky is to descend into an inferno." True. With *Brothers*, we confronted a vivid, intense display of emotion and suffering. Gene did his best, though, to make sure that we students emerged whole from that inferno. He showed us that Dostoyevsky was searching for God, as we should do. Gene helped us, through our reading and discussion and writing, to draw closer to the Father and the Savior. With Shakespeare, Gene did all of this even more effectively. *Hamlet* and *King Lear* were the perfect one-two combination for teaching the Atonement. Gene taught us that *Hamlet* illustrated the sad futility and ugliness of responding to wrongs with revenge and that *King Lear*'s Cordelia showed how forgiveness, the key Atonement component, can erase all wrongs in others and ourselves. Yes, I got it. ("Ah hah!") With *King Lear* and Gene, I saw that, more than anything, the Atonement brings us forgiveness and reconciliation. This is not just third-party debt payments. This is reconciliation and charity and loving embraces, despite willful harm inflicted by God's children.

I still relish these lessons and love literature in large part because of Gene, even though I was a physics major then and am an economist now. I enjoy calculus and data and charts and graphs, but Gene showed me how the art and craft of great literature can teach truth better than logic and can help one to *love* the truth, not just "know" it. Gene shared his insights with such steady and infectious enthusiasm (Bob Rees rightfully calls him an "enthusiast") that even math-loving, analytical me was drawn in—for good.

Gene also taught us to wrestle with profound and perplexing questions. He and the rest of the colloquium faculty stressed that in order to learn and to grow in knowledge, we must keep asking questions. They helped us to see the righteousness of questioning. At the same time, Gene and the others always taught us the crucial power of faith. The questioning in colloquium never challenged my testimony because we questioned with faith. We learned that faithless questioning runs the risk of spiritual starvation. And we learned that faith makes possible the integrity and charity needed for successful living. Gene did not question his faith; he faithfully questioned. And he showed us all how to do that.

When one questions, one might wonder about the scriptures and want to interpret them figuratively. Gene did tell us that he believed that the second biggest problem that people have with the scriptures is that they interpret them too literally. He then added that he thought the biggest problem was that people do not interpret the scriptures literally enough. They don't take literally its urgings for us to have the experiences in spirit that they point toward.

Gene could faithfully question because he himself lived the church's teachings and sustained the church's leaders. Family prayer, family scripture study, family night: Gene did all of these things. And I never heard him speak ill of the "Brethren." Overall, Gene was as true blue as any "conservative."

Sometime after colloquium, the Englands invited me, along with others, to their Kamas cabin at General Conference time. What a blessing to retreat from valley cares to mountain beauty and Charlotte and Gene warmth for a weekend. This, however, was not a vacation from living church teachings. We dutifully listened to conference, and, on Saturday night, we males made the trip to the nearest stake center to listen to the general priesthood meeting. Gene made sure of that.

Gene was an intellectual and a questioner, but dangerous? A threat to testimonies? Absolutely not. Anyone who thought that Gene was dangerous did not know him. (Besides, how could anyone who looked like a combination of Howdy Doody and Ted Koppel be a threat?) Gene was too smart, too much of a genius, to reject the gospel teachings or the church brought forth by Joseph Smith. And he generously shared his strong testimony of these things with thousands of others.

### HOME

Outside of class, I, along with many others, got to spend time at the England home, just north of the Marriott Center. This was easy to do because the door was never locked. In fact, don't tell Charlotte, but, more than once, I walked in, found no one home, helped myself to food, sat and read and relaxed, helped myself to more food and some drink, and then left without seeing anyone or getting anyone's permission. Such was the England home, an oasis and way station for vagabonds like me. As I think about that unlocked door, I wonder: can anyone argue with its generosity and genius? Most of us more selfish and duller folks in Provo lock our doors. Gene and Charlotte did not, and that made a world of difference.

I also had the privilege of actually getting invited to the England home. I dated Becky during my freshman year, which increased the number of those valued invitations. (I look back with fondness at those teenage dating times but also rejoice that each of us married so well a few years later.) During those visits, I learned that, on a personal level, Gene took time to learn about your beliefs, desires, and struggles. He radiated a pure interest in others. He genuinely wanted to know what you were thinking and why. If he disagreed, he would not judge; he just wanted to know why you held your opinions. I am sure that, if he were with us today and learned that I voted for "W" twice, he would, with a look of puzzlement combined with genuine warmth, quiz me on those choices in ways so that I would want to discuss them. I perhaps would shift the subject and ask why he believes that governments that lie about wars can be trusted to solve social problems or run health care. And we would be on our way to greater understanding through dialogue, or at least I would.

### COMMUNITY

In the community and the world as a whole, Gene's outreach to the needy is well known. The problems of the poor, the downtrodden, and the oppressed genuinely concerned him, and he generously shared that concern with others, as well as worked to help the needy himself. He started Food for Poland during that same year that I was in his colloquium. He gave heart and soul to this idealistic but spot-on cause. Looking back, I do not understand how he did it. Where did he find the time and energy to raise millions of dollars and ship millions of pounds of food and supplies to Poland while sharing so much with his students and with others? Such generosity *required* genius. I suspect that part of that genius was mobilizing and harnessing the generosity and time of others. Another payoff to that effort, though, was the example it provided to many of us. Gene actually devoted time, energy, and sweat to helping the needy instead of just talking about it. My international economics research has turned recently toward the problems and issues surrounding the world's poorest people. Gene's example from way back in my freshman year is one of the factors that have led me in this direction.

### GENE'S GENEROSITY

In the classroom, at home, and in the broader community of God's children, Gene selflessly told others to share, which takes more courage and charity than remaining silent. When Gene said, "Be generous, Mary," it was different and unexpected, but it was typical Gene and just the right thing to say. Gene had a unique, multifaceted, and ultimately Christlike generosity, enriched by a keen understanding of the human condition and the power of *agape*. I cherish the time I got to spend with Gene, the generous genius.

# Remembering a Truth About Gene

**STEPHEN BRADFORD**

Stephen Bradford recently tagged along with his wife, Jane, to live closer to amazing grandchildren under production in Berkeley, California, and Charlottesville, Virginia. Steve also dabbles in Mormon studies ventures at Claremont Graduate University, Graduate Theological Union, University of Virginia, and *Dialogue, A Journal of Mormon Thought*, while continuing to practice law (until he gets it right) with a California-based law firm.

In 1982, I had the privilege of presenting Eugene England with a student-decided award as the BYU Honors Professor of the Year, a recognition he genuinely seemed to value. While we students knew that Gene loved to "hole up" amongst mountains of thoughts and papers endlessly migrating and swirling around in his BYU office, we could sense that holding court among his students while sharing his contagious enthusiasm for literature, the gospel, and our potential was Gene's first academic love, and we loved him for it.

Indeed, my brother, Scott, and I remember spending some of our finest BYU hours absorbing Gene's wisdom in class, at church, and in his home (although it must parenthetically be acknowledged that Gene was significantly more compelling to us when one or more of his daughters was in the room; yes, Gene was interesting, but Katherine, Jody, Jennifer, Becky, and Jane were fascinating, especially when one or more occasionally deigned to allow for a date).

After graduating from law school in 1986, I serendipitously found myself living in the home of Gene's alter ego, Bob Rees, who was also my bishop in the Los Angeles 1st YSA Ward. One Sunday in a Westwood Chapel classroom, Gene appeared during an elders quorum lesson I was teaching. My adrenaline rushed as I observed him ever so slightly nodding his head while I mindfully taught what I thought to be the gospel according to Gene—complete with references to a progressing God, the church being at least as true as (and perhaps truer than) the gospel, and the need to redistribute our time and means to the poor among us.

Eventually, Gene raised his hand, and I eagerly awaited his approving exegesis on my persuasive gospel message. But to my chagrin, that's not what I seemed to receive. Instead, he called attention to nuances in our doctrine relating to deity, the church, and Christian service. He allowed for differing views on God's progression, that there's nothing more beautiful than the pure gospel of Jesus Christ, and that decisions about where to allocate time and resources were deeply personal. He even referenced someone I'd presumed to be a nemesis, the recently deceased Elder Bruce R. McConkie, to bolster his commentary.

After class, Gene came up and embraced me, asked how my mom and dad were doing, and enthused about a pupusas joint he planned to enjoy the next day with a daughter or two. I responded with appropriate interest; but as we spoke, I was still trying to figure out why he appeared to have allowed me to twist in the wind during class.

Some suggestions came to mind as he decamped for the parking lot. I recalled that Gene had always been remarkably consistent. I remembered that he had named his flagship journal of Mormon thought *Dialogue*, and that his mantra seemed to be this phrase, attributed to Joseph Smith: "By proving contraries, truth is made manifest."

My dashed expectation that Gene would join in lockstep behind my "liberal" take on the church and the gospel during elders quorum should have come as no surprise. Gene had invariably been about dialogue, proving contraries, seeking and (he hoped) finding reconciliation. Gene didn't want a discussion to just go in one direction and, in the process, overlook, intimidate, or exclude the thoughts of others.

In a word, I realized that Gene was about at-one-ment. He knew my elders quorum lesson couldn't function as well in that school of love we call church if I insisted on a unidirectional discussion or if I short shrifted those who may not agree.

In reflecting fourteen years later on his 1986 essay, "Why the Church is as True as the Gospel," Gene helpfully clarified what I felt that day in Westwood:

> We ... must constantly remind ourselves that the church is not a place to go for comfort, to get our own prejudices validated, but a place to comfort others, even to be afflicted by them. It is a revealed and effective opportunity to give—to learn and experience the meaning of the Atonement and its power to change us through unconditional love. It is a place where we have many chances to repent and forgive—if, for a change, we can focus on our own failings and the needs of others to grow through their and our imperfect efforts.

By refusing to acknowledge in elders quorum that the church is at least as true as the gospel, Gene had proven that the church is every bit as true as the gospel. His insights about the church are a major reason why I happily remain, and why I can joyfully and regularly celebrate the Atonement of Jesus Christ with a pleasantly diverse group of congregants who don't always think or act like me.

# Eugene England, Bodhisattva

**GIDEON BURTON**

Gideon Burton was a member of the English Department at Brigham Young University from 1994 to 2023 where he taught courses on Mormon literature, oratory, and film. A past president of the Association for Mormon Letters, he co-founded the Mormon Literature & Creative Arts database at BYU's Harold B. Lee Library, and as an editor at *BYU Studies* helped to publish special issues devoted to Mormon opera and Mormon film. He and his wife are the parents of four sons and live in Salt Lake City.

Bodhisattvas, according to Buddhist tradition, are enlightened ones who defer nirvana because their compassion compels them to remain behind to assist others. Statues of these demi-deities are recognizable across Asia by their graceful postures and cheerful faces.

When I learned about these saintly beings while studying India's religions, I thought of my former mentor and colleague, Eugene England. He would never characterize himself as someone any better than his sisters or brothers. But to me and many others, he played the role of bodhisattva, a kindly catalyst of enlightenment. At a very formative time for me, Gene was a most welcome mediating force, modeling to me how to be true both to my religious convictions and my intellectual inclinations.

I sat in his BYU office in 1985, newly returned from my mission to Montreal and having read *Dialogues with Myself*, eager to find out about the LDS Literature course Brother England taught. After showing me the syllabus, explaining how Mormon Literature was a living, evolving thing, and hearing of my interest in things literary, he looked at me and suggested, casually yet seriously, that perhaps I could be the author of some great work of LDS literature. This was Gene.

In my life I have needed mentors who think and feel deeply and who are energized (and not threatened) by the wide worlds of art, literature, and philosophy that so often inspire me, but which fall outside of my culture's habits and idioms—such as the truths I find in non-Christian cultures or in artistic traditions so foreign to my native Mormon milieu. And I have needed mentors who are unafraid to have convictions, follow commandments, prize covenants, and live a life of intentional discipleship. This is no easy combination.

In Gene, I found myself able to feel the intoxicating breadth of my religion's theology without getting drunk on peculiar-people pride or facile intellectualism. Through Gene's careful connectedness to community and Christ—so artfully articulated in his essay on "Why the Church is as True as the Gospel"—I have found myself able to be critical of my own life and the shortcomings of my community without abandoning personal faith or wrecking those critical human bonds without which none of it matters much anyway. He helped me to understand and to live Paul's admonition to the Ephesians to speak the truth in love.

Gene articulated the eloquence of Mormon belief and celebrated the ethical and intellectual foundations of our religion, even while simultaneously pinpointing the deep abyss between our faith's ideals and our own behaviors. I found from Gene that I did not need to be ashamed of my ignorance, nor of my desire to learn; of my sinfulness, nor of my desire to improve my faith. I know his voice did not speak to everyone, but it spoke to me, and throughout my adult life I have circled back to the principles that he taught that have helped me to believe in my religion and to strive for something better in myself and in my faith community.

But that could only happen if we are sobered into reflection upon our shortcomings. Gene was discomfiting, for he challenged us to revisit possible prejudices or dangerous folk-doctrines—the various ways we might be nominally but not fully Christian. He urged us to take more seriously Christ's atonement and Joseph Smith's revelations—all while in full view of human weakness and organizational imperfection. This was daring stuff. Yet Gene lived his life as a model of ethical pragmatism that did not shy away from either people or principles. I found that Gene unhid both my best and my worst selves while urging me on to be a better peacemaker and bridge builder.

Although Gene was genial to believers and to doubters, and of good cheer both to insiders and to outsiders, such kindness was not always answered in kind. This tends to happen when you call out things like entrenched racist attitudes within God's church. He used to tell me that he felt he was probably on track when his hate mail came in evenly divided between the orthodox and the heterodox. His good humor must have masked many pains, but he was steadfast in his charity. Only once did I ever see him take a defensive posture (which he followed up with quickly in a public apology). What dominated his demeanor was an openly charitable faith in others.

In the Lotus Sutra is found a description of the "Bodhisattva Never Disparaging," a figure who, out of an absolute conviction of the utter worth of every being, bows respectfully to all—even venerating those who mock or persecute him. This was Gene, never spiteful (as some of his supporters sometimes were in defending him). Gene made full allowance for others, especially those who tried to be his enemies.

And so, I look up to "Eugene Never Disparaging" without apology, grateful for his faith in reconciliation, happy for his mediating and tempering influence. He has invited me to look more deeply inward, more sympathetically outward, and to reach for a charity towards others that is not patronizing but courageous enough to wait and listen, to sympathize and humanize. How this pattern has proved itself for me throughout life!

In the mid-1990s I became Gene's colleague, also teaching the LDS Literature course at BYU. I always have my students read his essays and especially his breathtaking vision for Mormon art found in "Mormon Literature — Progress and Prospects." His view of the potency of Mormon artistic expression was built sturdily upon prophetic utterances from Joseph Smith, Orson Whitney, and Spencer W. Kimball, as well as upon Gene's own literary experiences.

Gene had engaged the world's literature and connected it to his faith; and through his own writing he made good on the words from Joseph Smith he so often quoted about truth being manifest as one proves contraries or tests apparent contradictions. Gene celebrated the written word for empowering us to address our worst, express our best, and identify compassionately with others. This is a vision that continues in his absence, made clearer and more forceful for having been so well lived and so well-articulated by him when he was among us.

Across from the staid stone buildings of Yale University I am writing today in the Atticus Bookstore Cafe. Gene was like Atticus Finch from *To Kill a Mockingbird*, only not fictional. He was generous and bright, and a fearless advocate. He stood up for the disenfranchised. He also checked himself, and us along with him, when tempted to simplistic liberalism, or away from grounding commandments and covenants. He admitted it when he was wrong. He tried again. He spoke the truth in love. And along the way, he taught so many of us to hold those oh-so-needed dialogues with ourselves.

Sometimes today I wonder what our friend Gene would say in the face of the debilitating political and cultural divisions that bring us down. Or I have wondered how he would stand up for those who remain ignored or patronized or harmed by those within the household of faith. But I already know how he would approach our times' challenges.

Gene was forever interpreting and acting toward others as though they had good intentions—even when evidence suggested otherwise. Even when his noblest efforts were actively misconstrued as disloyalty to the church, he remained "Eugene Never Disparaging," stepping aside from easy martyrdom, leaning into the good he could do wherever he was. He bloomed where he was planted, where he was transplanted, and even when trampled upon.

I have tried my best to imitate such deeply Christian traits—which is far harder than it sounds, especially when we may be animated by strong intellectual convictions or social causes, or if discouraged by entrenched cultural patterns resistant to constructive change. But Gene always gave others the chance to be right. Instead of being reactionary, as so many are today, he listened carefully, examined himself, and spoke the truth in love. Anyone could accuse him at such moments of being rhetorical or insincere, but there was nothing insincere about how his actions sobered me into being a more reverent believer, a more thoughtful writer, a more compassionate sibling to fellow sinners, and a more courageous and patient advocate.

# Appreciation of Eugene England

**CLAUDIA LAUPER BUSHMAN**

Claudia Lauper Bushman holds degrees from Wellesley College, BYU, and Boston University. She is the wife of Richard Lyman Bushman and they have six children. She has written several books and likes to do projects.

Gene was a young friend of my husband Richard's who reached out to all his friends to join in his projects. He drafted Richard to be book review editor when he began *Dialogue*, moving us closer to his sphere.

Gene was visiting with us once when we lived in Belmont, Massachusetts, and one morning we were walking in Harvard Yard, showing off the glorious buildings of the college and the area of Harvard Square. Our Cambridge group of aspiring housewives had been meeting for some time, sitting around discussing the challenges of our lives as unpaid laborers in a nation, in a church, and in families that did not encourage or appreciate us, weeping and complaining as toddlers crawled over our feet. After many meetings, I suggested that instead of suffering and complaining, we should undertake some projects to show what we could do, so we began to organize events and discuss issues, healthy and more demanding activities at which we were doing very well.

All of this was prelude to a great request I was planning to spring on Gene. I asked if he would entrust a group of smart, underutilized Mormon housewives to produce a special women's issue of *Dialogue.* Without asking for our credentials, requiring a plan, or in any other way questioning our abilities, Gene immediately and cheerfully agreed that we should do the special issue. Go ahead, we were told.

And so, our group of smart, domestic ladies began to discuss our *Dialogue* issue, to read and think about women's issues, to suggest ideas for articles, request them from other ladies, write some ourselves, and discuss and edit the materials that we had solicited. We were certainly busier and more cheerful about our lives than we had been before. Gene occasionally asked how we were doing, but he put no pressure on us. We worked away happily on it for a long time before it was finally completed, by which time Gene had turned over the editorship of the journal to Bob Rees. It took some discussion and negotiation with the new editorial team about how much freedom we had as special editors, which issues were most important, and how to handle differences of opinion on some of the articles. In the end, as Devery Anderson reported in his History of *Dialogue* series published later in the journal, our two groups eventually resolved our differences, and the published special "Pink" women's issue was very popular and celebrated by all.

Having learned to work together, our group undertook other projects, including *Exponent II*, the LDS feminist newspaper, which has now been published regularly for nearly fifty years. That too was a direct result of Gene's encouragement. His willingness to invite a group of housewives into the arena of serious thinkers changed all our lives.

Gene continued to work his magic over us. He called me one time and asked me to write a chapter for a collection he was editing titled *The Reader's Book of Mormon* (2008). I replied honestly that I really did not know anything about the scriptures and that I would get Richard to talk to him. "No," said he, "I want you to do it." My refusals were in vain. He would not let me out of doing it. So, I finally agreed to try, and spent many hours contemplating the scriptures before realizing that I did have something to say about them, and I did say it.

A lot of the writing I have done has been directly or indirectly influenced by Gene. Along the way he picked out a couple of paragraphs from things I had written. He quoted them and referred to them several times as good writing. I had never considered myself a writer at all and certainly not a serious writer, but his influence improved the care I took of my writing and made the final result better.

Thanks to Gene, I now know that I can do more than I ever think I can. I've always been a person who liked projects and could carry them through, thanks to my membership and training in a church of can-do people. And I'm certainly not as ambitious as he, who took on efforts that were too big, even for him. I salute him as one of the great influencers of his life and time.

# A Meeting of Minds

**RICHARD LYMAN BUSHMAN**

Richard Lyman Bushman retired from the Columbia University History Department in 2001. He is the author of *Joseph Smith: Rough Stone Rolling* and lives in New York City with his wife, Claudia Bushman. His most recent book is *Joseph Smith's Gold Plates: A Cultural History.*

Gene and I were good friends though of quite different temperaments. He was outspoken; I am soft spoken. I was continually telling him to calm down; he never paid heed. You go too far and ask too much, I would say—be patient. If you challenge the powers that be, you will lose all your influence. His reply: What good is influence if you don't use it? That came as a rebuke. Actually, his whole life was a rebuke to the complacent. He saw problems and dealt with them. Today, if he were with us, I would probably say the same thing: Be patient, and, as always, he would barrel on.

Why is it that despite his struggles Eugene England's influence is still felt so powerfully in Latter-day Saint intellectual circles? In the past couple of years, there have been significant biographies by Kristine Haglund and Terryl Givens. Both admire England while lamenting his inability to avoid conflict with the General Authorities to whom he was deeply loyal. Some of his battles seem inevitable; others he seems to have brought on himself. Is England relevant because he embodied in himself the state of scholars, artists, and thinkers in Latter-day Saint culture? As a body, are such folk both loyal and resistant just as he was?

What he lacked was philosophical distance. He was unable to step back and recognize the inevitability of a clash between university-based intellectual culture and authority-based church culture. He wanted too badly to merge the two, primarily by winning acknowledgment from authorities that his own campaigns growing out of current intellectual values were righteous. He suffered great pains because he truly loved the authorities and wanted their approval, but was convinced that his campaigns for equality, justice, and peace were also the cause of God.

Reading the two biographies is painful because they reveal England's anguish so poignantly. It fills his correspondence and shows through here and there in his talks and essays. He was devoted to a saintly life, not ostentatiously but as an outgrowth of his own kind heart and personal integrity. So fully was he committed that he thought surely he was innocent of any wrong against the church. Few live with more devotion to doing good, and that purity gave him confidence in the truth of his intellectual and moral campaigns. He was genuinely baffled when he was rebuked.

I think the buffeting he suffered served a worthy purpose. He opened space for others with similar sensibilities. I have mingled with many young Latter-day Saint scholars. For a decade or so, groups of thirty or forty graduate students would gather for "Faith and Knowledge" conferences. For a couple of days every other year, we would share notes on the tensions between our Latter-day Saint beliefs and what we were learning in the university. I soon realized that even the most faithful students felt stress, and many were lonely. More than one said after a weekend together that the little band we had gathered was about the only place they felt at home.

What that gathering did for a handful of graduate students, Eugene England did for two or three generations of rising intellectuals. He created a space where they could feel at home. They watched him take strong stands on current issues and then take the consequences when others felt he had gone too far. I hope thinking young Latter-day Saints have learned to be more cautious than Gene, but also to take courage from him. In Gene they have someone who held on to his principles while at the same time holding on to the church. There never was a question in his mind of taking leave of his faith. Faith was as essential to his being as was his resolve to make the world better.

Did England fight in vain? Did he go down to defeat without altering church culture? I don't think so. Latter-day Saint intellectual culture has never been more vital than it is today. We don't just have a handful of leading thinkers producing good work. We have scores and scores of well-informed, productive, ingenious working scholars and artists. We have a body of thinking people who know each other, who are fostering a rising generation, and who engage in projects to write and speak. We have never had more and better artists and composers. We have institutions like the Maxwell Institute, the Center for Latter-day Saint Arts, the Mormon History Association, Mormon Scholars in the Humanities, the Association of Mormon Letters, and on and on that focus on key issues and bring scholars together. Moreover, there is an ever-enlarging demographic of patrons of scholarship. They gather in fireside groups all across the country to listen to our intellectuals speak. If not authors themselves, these devoted onlookers want to know what is being thought and said.

All of this can be thought of as the legacy of Eugene England. He was, after all, the founder of *Dialogue*, our pioneer intellectual journal. There is nothing he liked better than to gather people to think and talk. He would be delighted with what has ensued since his passing. I think this generation of scholars has learned from Gene's sorrows too. Most are less adamant, less confrontational, more patient. They realize they can carry out their mission to think, write, and produce art without confronting church authorities. For their own reasons, they embrace their faith and know their commitment requires acceptance of hierarchical leadership. They don't require and seek church approval as Gene did. They find a space to do their work without confrontations.

Increasingly, Latter-day Saints today live an intellectual life—talking, contemplating, writing, doing art—without suffering life-sapping friction. I think they can live such a life in part because Eugene England cleared a space for them. He lives on, I believe, because of his good mind, more because of his good heart, but to a considerable extent because he was willing to suffer for what he believed. People learn from his writing, but still more are inspired by his life.

# On Shaking Hands with Gene England

**SCOTT CAMERON**

Scott Cameron is enjoying retirement with his wife, Christine, in Provo, Utah. He walks daily, reads daily, thinks about writing frequently, and gets around to it sporadically. He and Chris love their family, visit their children regularly, and follow their grandchildren's activities with devotion.

Homesick, I sat on my bed in Trancos Hall at Stanford on August 27, 1964, contemplating the mistake I had made. How had vanity and pride caused me to leave my home only to deposit me in a cinderblock room with two beds, two desks, and a single light in the ceiling?

It was hot for late August in Palo Alto, and the dorm did not have a swamp cooler. As I sat, a man appeared at the open door. My first thought was, "What great hair!" He almost looked like one of the Beatles. He had the most pleasant smile I had seen in weeks. As he extended his hand, he said, "I'm Gene England. Welcome to Palo Alto." As we shook hands, there was a demonstrable change in how I felt. Gene invited me to a meeting at Tresidder Memorial Union the following evening at 6 p.m. He said I would meet some of the other students who were members of the church. As a one-semester seminary dropout, I had certainly not intended to take an Institute class, but I felt so alone, I couldn't turn down an invitation from someone who made me feel so welcome.

When I arrived at Tresidder Memorial Union at 5:50 p.m., I found several students already gathered. They didn't look like people I had known in Salt Lake, but I reasoned, this was California. When other clean-cut types arrived, they seemed as reticent as I was to go inside. Finally, I recognized the friendly man from my dorm. He marched into the room and welcomed everyone there. He introduced himself as Gene England and referred to the poster reserving the space. He said that we were all students who were interested in organizing an LDS Institute class. One from the initial group said, "You mean this isn't a group interested in LSD?" Gene opened a box of donuts and said, "No, but you are welcome to join us."

Immediately, I thought, this man is perfectly "at home" with everyone. He genuinely wanted the students with apparent dyslexia to feel welcome. Several said thanks but indicated that they were not interested. When the meeting started, it was apparent that the upperclassmen who remained knew Gene very well and respected him. Gene outlined a format for the Institute class where students could talk about issues that they confronted in their courses. He then elicited suggestions for subjects we might cover. He indicated that the course would evolve over the quarter. He said the subsequent meetings would be held off campus at his home, and further suggested that we were welcome to invite our roommates or other friends we might meet in the next week.

This first meeting seemed fine, and the idea of designing the topics to be discussed interested me, but the subsequent meetings at Gene and Charlotte's home were like magic. I can still picture Gene and Charlotte's children—as happy to greet the students as were their parents. It was warming to see how Charlotte gathered her children and indicated it was time to read together, while Gene met with the students. I felt at home and cared for. The "gospel-related" discussions were open and free ranging. It was a marvel to see how Gene could get people to speak and then frame their comments into a question that others could react to. All felt open to express themselves and comment, and even comments I didn't agree with seemed worthy of consideration. I had never encountered a discussion leader who could so naturally start a discussion and sustain it while getting everyone involved.

Gene was working on his PhD in English and was friends with Mr. Sherman, my English teaching assistant. Gene and I met a few times, and he helped me to relate to Sherman, an urbane New Yorker, and perhaps helped him understand a young boy from Utah. Gene would frequently meet his Institute students on campus and at his home. He was interested in and concerned about all the undergraduates he and Charlotte taught and welcomed into their home. Gene and Charlotte were like a trusted older brother and beloved older sister—guides and friends. It was interesting the way they became a model for the way I wanted to parent. I hoped for the same warmth and goodwill to be in my home as I observed in the Englands' home.

Although Gene and the Institute director, George Pace, viewed the world through slightly different lenses, they trusted one another and provided balance and security for the undergraduates, young single adults and young married students they taught. The Institute was both a refuge and a discovery center.

On the death of President David O. McKay, Gene asked me to write a remembrance to be published in *Dialogue*. I was flattered, and his encouragement and gentle editorship led to "On Shaking Hands with David O. McKay." The confidence engendered by having my essay published was largely responsible for helping me lose my fear of the academic world.

It is interesting how lives meet and touch and part and meet again. Anthony Powell in his series of novels embodied it in metaphor by calling it "a dance to the music of time." After my undergraduate years, my encounters with Gene and Charlotte were sporadic. Although our meetings were less frequent, I followed with interest Gene's personal essays and other writings. During this period, his essay "Why the Church is as True as the Gospel," and the other essays in the book of the same name were like fresh air in my life. Because of our mutual friendship with Chuck and Kathy Petty, my wife, Chris, and I received periodic updates on Gene and Charlotte and their children. Frequently, I have offered prayers of thanksgiving for that first day when a kind and thoughtful man shook my hand and invited me to a meeting at Tresidder Memorial Union.

Years later, Chris and I moved into the Sharon East Stake where Gene and Charlotte were living. What a happy reunion! We have enjoyed the continued friendship of Gene and Charlotte and now Charlotte for over sixty years. Of course, we miss Gene, but we honor him in our thoughts and feel blessed to have Charlotte's continued friendship and loving example.

# Stepping off the Raft

**STEPHEN CARTER**

Stephen Carter is the director of publications for the Sunstone Education Foundation and host of the *Sunstone Podcast*. He is the author of *Mormonism for Beginners* (For Beginners Press), *Virginia Sorensen: Pioneering Mormon Author* (Signature Books), and the iPlates graphic novel series. He received the 2023 Smith-Pettit Foundation Award for Outstanding Contribution to Mormon Letters.

Eugene England died just a few days after I flew out of Utah heading to Alaska. Why Alaska, you ask? Because it was as far away as I could get from Utah. See, I was a good Mormon who already had two kids, so I couldn't go backpacking around Asia, tour Europe's hostels, or join the Peace Corps. But I had some big things to figure out. I don't think the phrase "faith crisis" was in popular use then, but that's what I was heading into. And Alaska, with its deep darkness, endless light, glacial silence, and crystalline cold, seemed like the perfect place to do it.

Officially, I went there to earn an MFA in creative writing with an emphasis in fiction. But every time I sat down to type, all I could write about was Mormonism. I couldn't help but delve into the past twenty-five years of my life and watch how religion had affected it. As I made those forays, I started to notice two forces fighting over me. Both were stories. One said, "The church is true." The other said, "The church is not true." They were like two rivers heading in different directions, both pulling at my raft, eager to interpret my life. The pull was strong in both directions, and I very much wanted to choose one and ride the strength of its current.

But something held me back from heading in *either* direction. It was the year I spent with Gene. You remember the old saying that people won't remember what you said but will always remember how you made them feel? In this case, I remembered what I *saw*. I spent a lot of time with Gene as his administrative assistant at what was then Utah Valley State College. One day, I was talking with him in his office when he started telling me how difficult it had been to hear what he had heard from men he believed were called by God. He was referring to the difficulties he had gotten into with general authorities that had eventually nudged him out of BYU. As he talked, I could tell that he was still struggling with the pain those events had caused. It was a tension he obviously wanted to be relieved of. But, oddly, I didn't see him trying to escape it. I didn't see him render judgments on the general authorities he had clashed with or even try to justify himself. Instead, I saw him dwell in the tension.

I had never seen anything like it before. It was such a striking experience that I decided to try applying it to my writing. Instead of following one river or the other, I got off my raft, stepped onto the land, and blazed a new path. This was much more difficult than I thought it would be. I started most of my essays thinking that I knew where they would end. And they were perfectly good endings—if you were following a river. But I was trying to do what Gene did, so I headed into the wilderness. There was no current to pull me along. No evident path ahead. Just my own efforts. I had to work and work and work on those essays. I had to spend way more time on them than they could possibly be worth.

As it turned out, every essay was a journey that ended only when I had changed—and changed in a way I could not foresee. I had to become someone new in order for an essay to become real.

I would say that Gene's example of dwelling in the tension has been the most significant defining force of my life; not because he taught me how to interpret reality but because he taught me how to *encounter* reality. And what I have learned is that it is an entirely different encounter, every single time.

Over the years, I've realized that the main value of this practice isn't that it is righteous or moral per se. I'm not a good person because I use it. Rather, its main value is that it helps me see more; it helps me feel more; it helps me experience more; it helps me connect more. I've learned that when I feel tension or pain, it's a sure sign that I am in a learning space. And the more tension or pain, the more possibility for learning. It's been especially helpful during the past few years when political tensions have run so high. Instead of feeling that I am surrounded by enemies, I feel surrounded by opportunities. When I say, "How could someone possibly think like that?" I no longer say it rhetorically. And, after some exploration, I find that the great majority of people are seeing useful things that can expand and enrich my thinking. It has helped me make, and keep, a lot of interesting friends.

I went to Alaska to get as far away from Utah as I could. But now, more than twenty years later, I am back in Utah. And Utah provides plenty of tension to dwell in. As does the church. So here I am. Surrounded by tension. Surrounded by pain. Surrounded by opportunities.

# A Pope Story: How One Person Brought Down the Berlin Wall

**JODY ENGLAND HANSEN**

Jody England Hansen is a writer, speaker, artist, activist, and advocate. She writes a regular blog for Exponent II. She often presents at Sunstone, on podcasts, and at conferences. She hopes her work inspires people to see how we all share the human experience that involves the possibility of great joy, and crushing burdens, and that the best thing we can do in this life is help each other along on our unique journey.

This is a story. It is not meant to be historically factual or told with the accuracy expected of a research paper, although it is about actual events. It is a story from my recollections. It's about Pope John Paul, my father, Gene England, and the Berlin Wall. There are many people who were heavily involved in the events of this story, but I will focus on the actions of just a few. When I think about the events from this story, especially during recent years, I see it as a movie—one of those independent films, made by someone who found out about a series of events that made a big difference in the world and is inspired to present them to a wide audience. If it had been made twenty years ago, Robert Redford could have played my dad. But he is too old for that part now. So, if you want to picture this story in your mind as an indie film while I am telling it, feel free.

In the fall of 1980, Dad was teaching at BYU. In November he was asked to be a last-minute replacement for one of the directors of the January Study Abroad program to London. We were all excited. This would be our first trip to London, and we knew we would also be able to travel all over Europe. Dad talked to the group in the orientation meetings about the opportunity this trip presented to learn and experience history and art and culture on such a level that our lives would never be the same. He said we could see it as a nice little extended sightseeing trip that included classwork and tests to get through, or it could be a time of enlightenment about ourselves, the world—and the difference we could make in it. Then he set about doing all he could to make that happen.

Dad had long taught and followed active non-violent resistance to conflict.

He was concerned with the prevalent attitude among the superpowers to use the massive buildup of military arms as a solution for supposedly keeping the peace. The main reason he saw that would never work was the teachings of Christ, and the lessons of the cycles of violence and destruction that occur throughout the Book of Mormon. He was deeply concerned with the way the Soviet Union was using force in Afghanistan and in Poland against the striking Solidarity Union. He saw a possible solution to the tense relations between the US and the Soviet Union was a massive exchange program. He proposed that one hundred thousand Soviet college graduates switch places with one hundred thousand US college graduates for at least two years. Let them experience life with their perceived enemies, which would lead to students on both sides seeing and learning from one another that they had more in common than they supposed. Since there was no sign that either government was interested in sponsoring such a program, he decided to do what he could. He started making arrangements for one of our weeklong excursion trips to be to the Soviet Union.

Dad had also been impressed with the way Pope John Paul had inspired such amazing events in Poland. In spite of the pressure from the communist government to remove religion from citizens' lives, there had been overwhelming response to his leadership when he was a cardinal in Poland. They even built a huge cathedral, most of it by members of the steel workers union that was the core of Solidarity. Now that he was pope, John Paul had called on his followers, who were suffering under tighter restrictions from a government trying to exert more control, not to allow circumstances to determine who they knew themselves to be. He asked them to stand tall and live the lives they were capable of, not stooping to violence, weakness, or destruction.

Dad was impressed with the non-violent activism of Solidarity and concerned that it was not receiving enough support from other countries, especially the United States, that could help it survive. He felt that supporting movements like this would be more effective in overcoming communism than providing guns and training to rebels in Afghanistan. I remember talking to him about it at the time. He shook his head a little, with this look of almost sad bewilderment. He said, "We are giving the rebels in Afghanistan terrible weapons and training them to use them against the Soviets. Their leaders see our society as their enemy as well. Can't our leaders see that we're training them to keep using violence to get their way, even after the Soviets are gone? It is dangerous to make alliances through violence." I think he could see that we, as a country, could suffer for those kinds of mistakes in ways we couldn't imagine. Given what happened in the War in Afghanistan, his concerns were prophetic.

He did want to go to Poland. I don't know what he thought he might be able to do or who he might be able to see, but he wanted to try to get there.

We were going to be traveling around Europe on the trains for about six weeks in the spring, and he tried to get visas that would allow us to go into Poland during that time. But Poland was closed tighter than ever, and we were unable to get the needed papers that would have allowed entrance. I don't think Dad ever gave up trying to figure out how he might succeed in getting there. After some of his actions to prioritize humanitarian concerns over rules during our week in Russia, I could imagine him thinking of possible unorthodox ways to enter—maybe "accidentally, on purpose" getting on the wrong train, or asking for a ride from someone who might "mistakenly" drive him across the border. This could be the action-figure part of the movie, maybe a James Bond type of dream sequence. But I think Dad knew that not even his look of "innocent" surprise and apology, "I'm sorry, I had no idea I was in the wrong country" could keep him out of jail if he were caught. So, he had to settle for bending as many rules as he could while we were in the Soviet Union.

We rode the train into Italy the first part of May. We stayed at youth hostels in Florence and Venice before going on to Rome. We were trying to cram as much art and architecture into our heads and Italian ice cream into our bodies as we could during the short time we had in each city. Rome was sunny, hot, packed with people, very noisy, and full of things to see. We planned to spend our last day at the Vatican. I remember standing with Dad as close as we could get to Michelangelo's *Pieta*. It was one of his favorite pieces of art. He loved the almost overwhelming expression of grace and courage in Mary.

We knew we would have time to listen to the Pope give his weekly address before we caught the train to Switzerland. Everyone gathered in the oval of the piazza, surrounded by the colonnades designed by Bernini, with the long rows of columns that seem to embrace those gathering in front of St. Peter's. We stayed in a group next to the huge pillar in the center of the piazza. Dad said he was going to try to get closer to the cathedral and told us he would meet us by the pillar. I decided to stay with the students. There were times when I was up to going with Dad when he wanted to get a little closer, because there is practically a guarantee that something will happen. But the crowds were packed tightly along the carpeted route that the Pope would be taking, and I didn't think it likely we would get much closer. Most of the students sat around the pillar, resting from a long day of walking. I climbed up on top of one of the short columns that surrounded the pillar so I could see the whole square and have a good view of the Pope.

As the Pope rode in, I was moved by both the adulation of the crowd and the love he showed to them. As the jeep moved slowly through the crowd, he stood and touched many of the hands reaching out to him. He was facing the cathedral as the jeep circled through the masses. Then, instead of continuing up to the building, the jeep circled around again. This time John Paul faced out, toward the columns, reaching out to those on the other side of the carpeted path. As he neared the end of this circuit, I heard several sharp popping sounds come from the right side of the crowd, then screams; the jeep suddenly sped away. I couldn't see the Pope anymore. It looked as though several men had climbed onto the car. A single man had run out of the crowd to the right, with a number of people running after him. When he got to the rows of columns, he stopped and turned, yelling something so loud I could hear it distinctly over the noise of the crowd. Then he disappeared as people surrounded him. They seemed so angry, I wondered if they might tear him apart.

This happened in a matter of seconds. I looked down at the others in our group sitting below me and said, "I think someone shot the Pope." We waited together as the impact of what had happened hit us and others in the crowd. Some were dispersing, but most seemed to move in together toward the front of St. Paul's, as if waiting to hear some reassurance about their beloved Pope.

I remember a group of nuns moving past us, holding on to each other and weeping. Then there was an announcement booming out from speakers around the square. The Pope had been shot but was still alive, and there was a plea for prayers for him. It also asked for prayers for others in the crowd who had been injured. The voice led those who wished in saying the rosary. One of my sisters noticed that Dad still had not joined us, and wouldn't it be weird if he were one of those injured? Since Dad was often where the most unusual or exciting thing was happening, that was not unlikely. Then he was there with us, a look of puzzled pain on his face, as if he were trying to understand something. "Dad, did you see?" "Yes, I was there. His hand was just about to touch mine." Dad reached his hand out, as though he were seeing it again. We could see red on his finger. He looked at it, a little frown on his face. "Dad, your finger is bleeding." "Yes, the bullet went by my head and clipped my finger." I looked at the right side of his face and saw it was red, as though his right temple had received a sunburn. The reality of the event seemed to be taking time to settle on all of us. We walked through the city to the train station. There were sirens and police cars speeding through the streets. We stopped by a police car where some officers were listening to their radio. Dad asked them questions, using the few Italian words he knew. They weren't able to tell us any news about the Pope.

We took the train to Geneva, Switzerland. We went to the mission home there to stay with our friends, Connie and Dave Bennion. The next morning, Dave brought back a European news magazine. The photo on the following page was on the cover. The reality hit full force. Dad wrote a piece for the *Deseret News* and called it in to their then columnist, his friend and former colleague, Clifton Jolley. He then started talking to people more about the effect this could have, not just on the Catholic Church, but also on the Solidarity

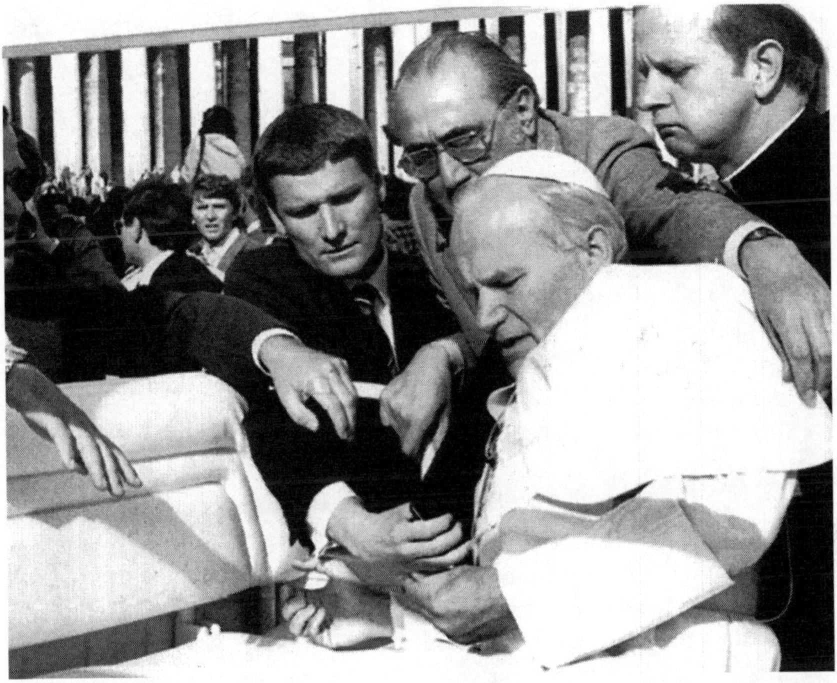

Eugene England in crowd at the May 1981 attempted assassination of Pope John Paul II in St. Peter's Square. The would-be assassin's bullet nicked England's finger as it whisked past his ear.

movement, and their non-violent resistance. He was also trying to find out what he could about the would-be assassin. Why did this man do this? Was he acting on the orders of a group or groups opposed to the pope's leadership?

Not long after we returned home to Provo, Dad and Mom held a meeting with us kids. They had decided to start an organization to gather donations of food and goods to send to people in Poland. They wanted to do what they could to support any non-violent resistance to resolve conflict. They asked us to support and help them. It was an opportunity to create the possibility of peace and choice in the world. It all began with us choosing to start Food for Poland.

It was after this that I think Dad developed the ability to alter time. He continued to teach and carry on with all of his responsibilities at BYU. He still worked on a number of boards, committees, and writer's groups. He had demanding church callings. He had a family who needed him. I now realize two of the main reasons he was able to make something happen in spite of all this: First and foremost—he had my mom. She was his essential partner in all things, and she is the one who made things work. I don't think anyone will ever completely know how much they relied on one another for the life they created together. It was truly a partnership.

The second reason—he brought his commitment to everything and everyone in his world that was important to him, and he invited all of us to be a part of it. He asked his family, his friends and colleagues, students and ward members, next-door neighbors, and those who lived on the other side of the world. Everyone he came into contact with was invited to participate. So, he wasn't trying to apportion a certain part of each day to all the important parts of his life. It all overlapped in a large interactive community. Yes, there were plenty of times that many of us just wanted Dad to have a simple commitment-free life to share with us. But if he did that, he wouldn't be Dad.

Many people tried to dissuade him from undertaking such a project, arguing that he didn't have time, he had other obligations and very valid commitments, he didn't have money or connections to start a charitable organization, it was not his place as a professor at an LDS university in a conservative town to be gathering and sending donations to striking union workers, most of them Catholic, who lived in a communist country on the other side of the world. Some called him a traitor, and he even got a death threat. But I think the hardest reason for him to accept was: "It won't make any difference. No matter what you do, it won't change anything." It must have been discouraging. Dad continued on.

Things started to happen. We created a letterhead and sent out mailings. Booths at BYU and other campuses helped raise a small army of volunteers. Dad talked with everyone he knew who could help him with all the things he did not know: organization questions, tax-free status, sponsorship, how to make contact with national celebrities who were of Polish descent, how to get news media coverage, how to store donations of food until they are shipped and how to ship them, what donations are most needed, how to know they will reach the people they were intended for, etc.

I won't take time to tell how everything happened. I will just touch on a few things. Dad got ahold of phone numbers for the leaders of Solidarity. I remember him asking me to be on the extension when he made a phone call to Solidarity's vice president asking what they needed. The answer: "Milk for the children. The children do not have food. And soap." I wondered why they would need soap if they were starving. Dad responded, "Can you imagine how hard it would be to go into meetings to negotiate with oppressive government leaders who had the power to keep you from getting milk for your children, and you had to go in dirty clothes and smelling bad? It is another way the government is chipping away at their dignity."

Dad kept calling people until he had connections all over the United States. Donations were made of all kinds and all sizes. He helped arrange unprecedented cooperation between Latter-day Saint and Catholic churches. Mormon missionaries and Catholic parishioners gathered to help load goods for shipment. All of this helped develop the current Church Humanitarian Services Department. We were able to send a representative with airlift shipments to guarantee they were received by Solidarity. Governor Matheson declared a statewide fast day for Poland, asking people to donate to Food for Poland from the money saved on meals during that fast.

With more donations and shipments, the Solidarity Union continued to strike, and survive. In October 1983, Lech Walesa was awarded the Nobel Peace Prize. Solidarity was making a difference in the world. Economic conditions eventually forced the Jaruzelski regime to negotiate. That led to parliamentary elections, and the establishment of a non-communist government.

November 1989: The Berlin Wall came down, without guns, without bombs—with celebration on both sides of the wall.

People have told me how unusual Dad was as a person with so many inherent abilities to do all the amazing things he did. However, I have come to see that things didn't just come easy or fall into place for him. There were no extraordinary genes in this extraordinary man. He came with pretty much the same capability for success or failure that most of us do. He consciously set out to create himself as someone who makes a difference in the world. I am fortunate to have been one of the people who was able to witness and experience some of this with him. What he learned to do, I can learn to do. True, the world will never see another like him. The world will also never see another like me or any of us. We are each that unique in what we can choose to offer.

There are many morals to this story. Here is one: You are most powerful when you create reasons to do things and know you created the reasons. Dad could have listened to any of the reasons that were given to him—no time, money, obligations, loyalties, you can't, it won't work, it's not your place. Instead, he chose to make up his own, and it was a reason that was bigger than anything he came up against. Let's call that reason world peace. The power to create a reason that big is the power to tear down walls.

Who is the one person who tore down the Berlin Wall? It is Pope John Paul, it is Lech Walesa, it is my dad, my mom, my sisters and brother and me. It is each person in Solidarity, each person who donated, fasted, and prayed, or took a stand. The wall was not brought down by millions of people. It was brought down by one person, hundreds, thousands, millions of times.

# A Leap into the Dark

## GEORGE MARK ENGLAND

Mark England is the father of four children, an artist, and the owner of Dolcetti Gelato in Salt Lake City. He is married to Kari England. He confesses, "Most of my time is spent confused and overwhelmed as I try and make sense of everything. The rest of my time is spent in absolute joy and wonder at how amazing life is."

My father grew up with parents who had a definite plan for him to become a great leader in the Mormon church. He bent over backward not to have a plan for me, but rather to give me the freedom and space to be who I wanted to be. What is important is that he never pressured me to be something or someone other than what I wanted to be. While he had high expectations, I never felt the need to perform or do anything or be a certain person just to make him happy. In retrospect, he may have done this to a fault, since at times I needed him to give me more direction, which may have led to my not feeling as "successful" as I might otherwise have felt. At least, I had his example of hard work, dedication, faith, humor, and integrity to guide me.

At times, dad spent too much time at work, fulfilling callings, studying and writing, or serving others, which was difficult for me, since I wanted some support as the only son in a family with five girls. Also, he tended to be a little formal when he was trying to connect with me. But the fact is that he did connect in his way, for example, taking me to see *2001: A Space Odyssey* when I was ten, and giving me a copy of *Moby Dick* when I was twelve. I did not understand them, but I got the message that there were serious, meaningful lings in life and I was worthy of them. Pay attention.

Sometimes I could tell if he was disappointed in me, but he was far more patient with my failures and hardly ever told me when I was making a mistake or what I should do with my life. During my formative years in Minnesota, I saw him mostly in the role of branch president, which was a natural extension of his role as a father. The way he handled both appeared to me seamless. That is, he treated the branch like his family and was consistent in this behavior, although, understandably, at times, I felt like visitors and strangers got more of his attention than I did. My parents set an example of generosity with their home that their children have all emulated.

I don't remember ever questioning Dad's ability or wisdom because he never did anything that would give me reason to question either. I don't know how he did it, but I never felt like he had to boss me around, even though I knew that he wanted or expected something of me. I believe the first job of parents is to show unconditional love and acceptance of their children, to love as our heavenly parents love us. Dad loved and accepted me for who I was, no matter how much I failed. I miss that so much, especially as I have endured deep trauma, rejection, and loss.

I believe it is a universal wish of all sons to see their father as perfect, wise, and strong. With only a few minor exceptions, that is how I saw my father. Like all fathers, he was embarrassing to be around when I was a teenager. He was clueless about some things. He had a goofy dance style that defied description, except that it was completely self-expressive. Perhaps that came from the modern dance class he had taken at the University of Utah. Seriously, who can boast that their father, who grew up on a dry farm in Idaho, took modern dance as a teenager? What kind of person does that? That one bit of information is enough to show how truly unique my father was.

One of my earliest memories of my father leaping into the dark happened when I was nine. It is a memory that cemented forever my vision of him. Our family, along with ten other families, had purchased 160 acres of redwoods and oaks above Palo Alto that we used for weekend getaways. The place, called "Bearmont," was full of adventure and possibility, which was perfect for a young boy. I have vivid memories of exploring the streams, finding salamanders and banana slugs, building fires, and watching my father work on the various projects that brought in water, roads, and sleeping quarters.

One weekend, all the men and boys went up for a sleepover. We decided to play capture the flag, which is my favorite outdoor game. Being in three-hundred-year-old redwoods with highly uneven terrain and it being almost pitch-black at night, this was a perfect place to play the game. We set up the dividing line through a clearing where the road ended and built a huge bonfire in the middle as the only source of light, which made everything even more exciting and difficult, since visibility was limited to the bonfire that threw shadows against the massive redwoods. The clearing was illuminated, but the minute you left the clearing, you dropped into the darkest night you could imagine. The towering trees blocked out any starlight or moonlight and absorbed any reflective light. The ground was extremely uneven, strewn with treacherous fallen logs, poison oak, and twisted branches.

We divided into two teams, the fathers and young boys on the uphill side of the clearing and the older boys on the other side. About forty feet into their side, the ground dropped five feet down into the dark underbrush, and then another fifty meters beyond that, it quickly dropped down a very steep slope into a canyon.

After and hour, neither team was able to prevail. Suddenly my father bolted across the line and grabbed the opponent's flag. Instead of running back toward his own side, which would have ended with him being caught, he kept going across enemy territory, leaping down the slope, plunging into the darkness of the forest. With the older boys, flashlights in hand in hot pursuit of him, we waited and listened breathlessly. Time passed and our anxiety grew. Where was my father? What had happened to him? I pictured him running through the redwood forest, through underbrush, over fallen logs and branches in pitch blackness down steep slopes and with no flashlight. After what seemed an awfully long time, he emerged on our side, striding out of the darkness, the enemy's flag in hand, having somehow found his way over and through the dark, treacherous terrain. He was all scratched up and dirty, appearing in my boyhood memory like some mythic hero.

This whole event earned the respect of all the other boys and became legendary among our group. For me, it confirmed that my dad was the perfect hero, the kind that ventured into the wild unknown and came back to tell about it, much like the stories of Beowulf and Grendel he would tell with great drama. This image lasted throughout my youth as I gradually had to deal with what it took to separate and distinguish myself from my father. Dad's whole life was characterized by his willingness to leap into the dark, deliberately, methodically, calmly. Whether it was writing letters to general authorities or trying out new programs as a bishop to help struggling members of a branch or ward, or taking numerous groups of students on adventures to England, he never played it safe.

One of the biggest challenges of my youth was going home teaching with my dad. He would take me across the rolling hills and farmlands of rural Minnesota to visit what seemed to me strange, lonely people around whom I felt very uncomfortable. Most of the time they were old, poor, uneducated, or uncultured. At least, I saw them that way. It took many hours and was not what I wanted to be doing on Sunday afternoons. While I considered my dad as superior to all of these people, he never acted so and, in fact, treated them with love and dignity, relating to them the same way he related to everyone—the way God sees us—as his children, loveable and fully capable of further light and knowledge.

Unlike some intellectuals, my dad was humble. He tended to accept people for who they were and saw everyone—including those who mistreated him—as having the capacity for goodness. This is why he was so effective in relating to others, including the marginalized who sought out his counsel. This was also why he was so effective in persuading others, including me. I'm sure I resisted at times, but somehow my dad prevailed in getting me to go someplace or do something without forcing or arguing with me. He was so gentle, centered, and strong in his convictions and purposes that resistance was not something I considered. I don't remember questioning his wisdom or plans, because he invited dialogue rather than contention.

This explains why he kept engaging with general authorities and others in an attempt to create dialogue on important subjects, including controversial ones, even when it led to discomfort or stress for him. For example, when my father asked for advice on starting *Dialogue: A Journal of Mormon Thought*, one church leader warned him that if he did, he would never have any high calling in the church. What this leader didn't understand about my father was that he was not motivated by power, position, prestige, status in the church, or money. What he cared about was seeking truth, obtaining knowledge, engaging in meaningful dialogue, and serving others. The only award I know he was proud of was the Honors Professor of the Year award chosen by the students in 1982 and again in 1988. In our home he did not exercise his priesthood in a domineering way. One could say that he was like gravity, an invisible but stable influence on all of us. He would lead Sunday dinner debates but never dominate them. When he died, all of us lost that invisible center of gravity we felt in his presence.

I have only one memory of him being impatient with me, and that was when I was thirteen. I can think of hundreds of times he should have lectured me or told me what I should be doing instead of the stupid thing I was doing, but he didn't. This strength and patience became even more pronounced in the last six months of his life when he lay dying of cancer. After a lifetime of choosing to leap into the dark adventures of life, taking different jobs, following his intellectual pursuits, traveling, filling church callings, and strengthening relationships, this was his last leap into the dark, one that chose him. Usually, when people are under stress, their true character comes through. Even though my father was in great pain and suffered loss of control of his life, he chose to remain the same patient, gentle person I knew my whole life. His passing left a huge hole in our family and community, just like Jimmy Stewart's character in *It's a Wonderful Life*, which was his favorite movie.

As I progress through life raising children and trying to be a good father and husband, I see myself in the shadow of my Dad. He gave me many gifts, including the space to choose my own path, but the greatest gift he gave me was acceptance of myself. His example and essays inform how to treat others that I impulsively want to reject. I often think about what my father would do in situations in which I find myself. Hardly a month goes by that I don't meet someone who tells me what a great influence my father had on his or her life and how they felt accepted and loved by him. As a teacher, writer, colleague, or friend, he brought light to others by being willing to live by light and, when necessary, to leap into the dark.

# A Home Away from Home

**NICOLE GHARDA**

Nicole Gharda attended London Study Abroad with Eugene and Charlotte England in 1998 and rented a room in their home for the following three years, until she graduated from BYU with a BA in English. She went on to get her master's in English at the University of Virginia in 2002, after which she taught for three years at a Jewish day school in Washington, DC. She has now settled in Long Beach, California, where she resides with her husband and daughter, Charlotte, and teaches English to high school students.

As the plane embarked on its descent into LAX, I looked down in dread at the brown flatland of Los Angeles—such a disappointingly stark contrast to the rolling green terrain that I had grown to love in England. Worse than the lackluster landscape, though, was this sinister sense that I was descending into a place I was expected to greet as my long-lost home when it in fact felt like the furthest thing from it. *This isn't my home, these aren't my people,* looped continuously through my mind. As I bemoaned the idea of resuming life in America, I reflected back on a conversation I had had with my Aunt Katherine before leaving for London to join her father, Eugene England, on the BYU Theatre Study Abroad program.

"I'm so happy you're going to London with Daddy. It's going to change your life." At the time, I assumed she was referring to the opportunity to engage with the vibrant art and theater scene in London. And to a certain extent, she did. But by the time I was touching down in Los Angeles at the end of my spring term on Gene's program, I realized my life had changed in a much more profound way. In going as far from home as I had ever been, I had found my intellectual and spiritual home.

Not only did Gene challenge us intellectually unlike any other teacher I had had before (the B+ I got in his Shakespeare class being the lowest grade I got in non-PE courses at BYU), he also engaged us to think critically about morality and ethics. He asked us to think about the pain of easily maligned Shakespearean characters like Malvolio in *Twelfth Night* before participating with the rest of the audience in unthinking laughter at Malvolio's expense. He asked us to consider the wisdom in Hamlet's parting words to "let be" while observing the consequences of the revenge plot on a stage littered with dead bodies. He asked us to question the drive for spectral evidence as we watched Iago manipulate Othello to rely on its fabrication to undo his trust in Desdemona.

But his moral lessons extended beyond Shakespeare and our classroom. He participated fully in the local ward's meetings, giving a fireside exploring his own memories of the church's evolving position on Black members and the priesthood because growing numbers of its congregation's new converts felt they had been blindsided when friends questioned them for joining the church given its history of racism. He gathered us together to break the news that an older woman who had enrolled in our program with her husband had passed away in the night and encouraged us to share our memories of her vivacious spirit. And when he sensed my eagerness to join him in London again, he invented a fiction about employing me as his TA to cover the cost of my housing and theater tickets. Sure, I developed a *Lamplighter* newsletter modeled after the work done in years past by his daughter Jane and made announcements to students about day trips I was taking should they care to join me, but another student was grading the papers.

In spite of his and Charlotte's generosity, my parents often let it escape that they worried Gene would lead me astray from my faith. I never understood where their fears came from beyond their quickness to judge his participation in "fringy" Mormon associations like Sunstone. If anything, when I was lucky enough to rent a room in the England home during the rest of my time at BYU, it was my conversations with Gene that made me hesitate to jump ship. I would come home from my religious education courses feeling disillusioned by professors pushing a theology of privilege, encouraging students to take pride in being members of the church in America as a sign of their valiance in the pre-existence. As I shared my frustrations with the implications of this theology over dinner, Gene did not readily agree and confirm my angst as I expected; he helped me wrestle with it myself by playing devil's advocate, forcing me to dialogue directly with the ideas in a way I lacked the courage to do in class and in person.

"You mean, you don't think you did something to deserve being born into a Mormon family in America?"

"Well, no, I don't! How can someone try to imply that something you can't control, like the circumstances of your birth, arises from choices you made before this life? What is that supposed to mean for people who were born in poverty or in politically unstable countries? You don't believe that, do you, Gene?"

As my frustration mounted, he was steadfast in his refusal to give me the easy support and approval I sought and instead would chuckle. "It doesn't matter what I think. This is one of those questions you have to answer for yourself."

Instead, as I spent long hours waiting for the dial-up modem hooked up to the basement computer where I emailed friends back home, I would grab copies of Gene's books to pass the time. I remember the reassurance I found in "Letter to a College Student" in his personal copy of *Dialogues with Myself: Personal Essays on Mormon Experience*. The humility he expressed there—empathizing with frustrations the student had expressed about the narrowmindedness of fellow congregants while also openly admitting that he had been guilty of some of the same behaviors himself—was consistent with the ideas he expands upon in *The Church is as True as the Gospel*, only here he was speaking to the specifics of someone in my particular situation and stage of life.

As I helped Charlotte with the preliminary stages of organizing Gene's letters and writings in preparation for a library collection, I marveled even more at the strength I observed living daily in his home from 1998–2000, during the years immediately following his dismissal from BYU and the year before his death. As I struggled to understand what could possibly justify pressuring the best professor I had been blessed to learn from to leave, not to mention other especially conservative moves under President Bateman's leadership (among them a controversy about the so-called "eroticism" of some of Auguste Rodin's art when BYU was blessed with an exhibition of his work), I never heard Gene complain. He never sought to dissuade me from my continued enrollment, even when I myself felt frustrated and limited by incursions on academic freedom as they affected my ability to learn as a student seeking knowledge.

No, somehow, he helped make one of the brightest moments of my life living in his home during perhaps one of the darkest times for him. On more than one occasion, he invited me to join his writing group, which included another favorite professor, John Bennion, and a favorite writer, Levi Peterson. I walked downstairs to attend regular concerts with traveling and local folk musicians in the Englands' living room. And I found an important mentor not only in him but also in Charlotte. Her influence was so significant that I named my first and only child after her—a decision which involved bucking the tradition of five generations of women named after my great-great-grandmother. Watching the beauty of Gene and Charlotte's marriage as they danced elegantly to Nat King Cole and engaged fully in their life with one another formed an important image of the kind of healthy partnership I was determined to find in my own marriage, even if it meant I wouldn't marry until long after most Mormon women do.

When it was time for me to move on from my home with the Englands to attend graduate school, I started down a path that led me to discover many years later that I no longer had a home in the church, either. When I think of Gene's steadfast faith, part of me feels weak for leaving. But while I may have parted ways with his theology, I have never parted ways with his intellectual influence or moral guidance. As I teach literature to high school students in Long Beach, each year I share with them something he shared with me—Kenneth Burke's assertion that literature ought to provide us with "equipment for living." In the wake of a pandemic that has left teachers worried primarily about the social and emotional learning needs of students who have been devastated by widespread death and social isolation, I remind the students at my high school focused on careers in engineering, civil justice and investigation, and health and medicine that though they will likely not major in English, reading literature like that which Gene taught me to love will equip their hearts and souls to be ethical, moral human beings. Because all of us deserve to feel we have found our intellectual and moral home, no matter where we happen to inhabit this globe.

# A Stranger and You Took Me In

**SUSAN LINDSAY GONG**

Susan Lindsay Gong holds master's degrees in English literature and instructional psychology and technology. She is a language educator, having taught English to teachers in several countries in Asia and Chinese to American students. She was the first coordinator of the Utah Chinese Dual Immersion Program and is the author and series editor of *Step-by-Step*, an award-winning program of more than eighty illustrated elementary readers for Chinese-language learners.

In January 1979, having recently returned to BYU from a mission in Taiwan and feeling a little adrift, I was hired as the administrative assistant for the BYU Honors Program, then directed by Professors Gary Browning, Clayne Robison, and Gene England. Each of these talented professors bore with me through some early missteps, coached me toward professionalism, and taught me about purposeful, transformative leadership. I'm indebted to each; but Gene and Charlotte England, with amazing generosity, mentored me, as they have so many others, by enfolding me into their enchanting family at a critical transition in my life, and helped launch me on the impossible-to-have-foreseen adventures of life.

It began with a simple act of hospitality. Shortly after I started working in the honors program, Gene invited me to attend the legendary soirees he and Charlotte hosted in their Provo home. Great food and fascinating conversation were magnets drawing interesting people together. Sir Arthur Henry King shared anecdotes from his service in the British Council as well as insights about the theme of grace in *King Lear*. James Arrington and Gene swapped surprising stories about Brigham Young. These stimulating, serious, hilarious, joyous, faith-filled discussions opened new worlds to me.

It's funny, the details we remember. An enormous Christmas tree dominated the living room of the England home the evening I attended my first soiree that January. It seemed so eccentric. Christmas trees were to be taken down at the first of the year. In February, decorated with valentines, the tree still graced the room. In March, by then a little shabby, it was decked out in shamrocks. I don't recall with certainty, but the tree may have even made a final feeble attempt to brighten April's Easter celebrations. Like so many things about the England home, the tree was whimsical, imaginative, and unconventional. The home had been built using bricks rescued from demolished buildings, the England children having cleaned each brick by hand. Charlotte set a beautiful table with pieces of fine china in a mix-and-match variety of floral patterns. Charming.

Charlotte—warm, effervescent, creative, articulate, authentic, and intelligent, a woman beautiful at every age—was clearly the heart of their home. She supported Gene in his many causes and pursuits; he supported her creative and business ventures. Their eyes twinkled when they looked at one another. There could not have been a charismatic Gene without this incredible Charlotte. To my young eyes, they were a perfect match.

A few months into the semester, Gene asked if I would like to be the teaching assistant for a survey of western humanities section of the Honors Freshman Colloquium that he, Noel Reynolds, and Karen Lynn were slated to teach fall semester. Colloquium was a relatively new honors program offering. Three distinguished professors shared responsibility for content and instruction. The course format was famous for its stimulating intellectual give and take. I jumped at the chance to be a part of it.

Gene was a master teacher. More than forty years later, I still remember his lectures on a variety of topics. No matter how obscure the texts, he succeeded in making them relevant and interesting to his freshmen students. For example, *Sir Gawain and the Green Knight*: What is the author's central message? What Christian themes are at play in the poem? What does it say about mercy and justice? Do elements of the chivalric code have relevance today?

Theodicy: How can evil exist in a world created by a loving god? What is the role of moral agency? Is there purpose in suffering? Can we trust a god who allows pain? Gene encouraged us to think deeply about these impossible questions. In his lectures he systematically outlined classic Christian responses to the problem of pain. In conclusion, he reminded us that, as professed disciples of Christ, we each have an obligation to alleviate suffering wherever we find it in the world. He finished bearing a personal testimony of the goodness of God and the promise that we can feel his love even in a fallen world.

Gene taught his students to create original, consequential theses, state them succinctly, and defend them with careful logic and pertinent examples. He often quoted from student papers to share the best examples of vivid prose and well-reasoned argument. Students beamed when he singled out their paper.

Gene and Charlotte, devoted romantics, made introductions and facilitated opportunities for relationships to blossom. When Gerrit Gong—the man I'd corresponded with for years and in whom I was more than a little interested—turned up in Provo without warning, I confided my hopes to Charlotte and Gene. The Englands, I learned, were old friends of the Gongs, having known one another in Palo Alto many years before. As it happened, the Englands were planning to invite the Gongs to their cabin on the Weber River that very week. Would I be interested in coming along as a friend of the family? Absolutely! They thus provided a genial, relaxed setting in which to meet Gerrit's family. It was on a memorable, unhurried walk in the forest beyond the England family cabin that I had my first heart-to-heart with my future mother-in-law.

When Gerrit finally proposed marriage, Gene and Charlotte hosted a tongue-in-cheek "candle passing" ceremony—the sentimental sorority tradition announcing an engagement—inviting the colloquium faculty and their spouses and other friends to celebrate.

A year later, Gene and Charlotte directed the BYU Study Abroad program in London. Gerrit and I were then living in Oxford. Wanting to give students experiences beyond visiting museums and attending concerts and plays—encounters that would help them understand better the lives of English people—Gene called one day asking if it might be possible to arrange short homestays for his BYU students with local church members. Students would pay a small fee for room and board for the weekend. The amount would be enough to compensate the members for their time and costs and a little extra. The ward bishopric agreed to the plan, and we went about matching students to interested families. Oxford ward members signed up enthusiastically. For many, even a little extra cash would make a big difference. Then doubts set in. What if these American students wanted to phone home? Would they be willing to eat bangers and mash? Would the students trash their homes? The potential hosts had all seen American movies and weren't sure they wanted such teenagers in their homes. With reassurances that all costs would be covered and that these students would be on their best behavior, the walk-a-mile-in-my-shoes homestays went forward and—as Gene had envisioned—were a positive learning experience for all.

Gene and Charlotte made it their business to be generous and supportive mentors and friends to countless strangers who crossed their paths over the years. I am deeply grateful for their many, many kindnesses to me.

# Witnessing Reconciliation

**JAY GRIFFITH**

Jay Griffith explores ideas and facilitates dialogue and relationships. He co-founded and manages the monthly discussion groups, ThinkAgain-FaithAgain.life and the advisory board of Faith Matters. By profession, Jay designs, art directs, writes, and creates. Preoccupations include trying to be like Jesus, trail running, reading widely, attempting to write poetry, and being with and caring for nature—including humans. He and his wife, Jane, are in close familial relationships with three grown children, two daughters-in-law, two grandchildren, two cats, three chickens, and one adored rescue dog.

At a time when political and religious self-righteousness is tearing our institutions apart, reflecting on Eugene England's life and personal encounters with him are not just timely but critical. His life speaks volumes about Christian discipleship through thoughtful advocacy without rancor and recrimination.

About halfway through my life, I met Gene England for the first time. To be clear, I only met Gene through his writings and those who knew him personally. I am now nearly sixty-five years old, and it seems fitting, if not ironic to some, that at the halfway point in my life it was my politically conservative ward member, client, and friend, Rob, who introduced me to Gene through Gene's book, *Why the Church is as True as the Gospel*. In the early nineties, while we were in Provo on business, Rob took me by Charlotte and Gene's home. Several years earlier he had met the Englands due to taking a wrong turn off the BYU campus and inadvertently discovered their home—a home he found so striking in its pioneer beauty and simplicity that he felt compelled to knock on the door and ask for a tour. He was delighted to find, as he was graciously taken through, that he was meeting the author of that book as well as Gene's remarkable wife, Charlotte.

Many years later my wife, Jane, and I found ourselves sitting in that same lovely home with Charlotte, witnessing what felt like a miracle. The pleasure of meeting and getting to know Charlotte personally was something I had never considered, but it felt at the time, and still feels so in retrospect, that our Heavenly Parents were working their at-one-ment, and that I was just a fortunate bystander blessed to help facilitate a degree of healing.

**A LITTLE BACKGROUND:**

In 2012, James (Jim) Wilson McConkie, the nephew of Bruce R. McConkie, moved onto our street in East Millcreek, Utah. We soon became fast friends with him and his wife, Judith. Kind, intelligent, faithful, and liberal-leaning, they are easy to love. Jim spent much of his time growing up in the company of two general authorities—his Uncle Bruce and his Uncle Joseph B. Wirthlin. Jim's father had passed away when he was seven, and these two apostles took a keen interest in him, each telling Jim to take the other uncle's beliefs and admonitions with a grain of salt. Elder Wirthlin was a theologically liberal Republican and Elder McConkie a theologically orthodox Democrat. It's no wonder Jim walks such a thoughtful, faith-filled path, a path similar to what Gene's life and writings point us to.

Less than two years before meeting Jim, I had become friends with a remarkable humanitarian-minded couple who invited me to a monthly discussion group they had formed in Salt Lake City called ThinkAgain. I loved the vibe of those who attended and enjoyed exploring important topics in their home. They eventually moved to Bountiful and group members, Mark and Dawn England, began hosting this gathering in their home in Sugarhouse. Mark is Gene's son and through him, I eventually met Charlotte. In the spring of 2013, I was asked if I would lead the group by the person managing it. With some trepidation, I agreed.

Not long after, I arranged for a ThinkAgain discussion on navigating Mormon history and faith crises, a topic of increasing interest to me as well as many other Latter-day Saints. I asked Jim if he would be willing to participate and he graciously agreed, as did Andrea Maxfield, a friend, and assistant to then LDS church historian, Richard Turley.

It was a truly remarkable evening. Jim, a talented attorney and longtime close friend of LDS historian Michael Quinn, knew well the difficult historical issues of the church. He beautifully held an empathetic space for the thorny and complex questions and understandable pain of those struggling. He also offered unapologetic historical context and theological explanations that provided opportunities for belief within our complex and messy history.

Afterward, Dawn England suggested we form an additional monthly group to explore challenging topics related to the Mormon faith. With some reticence, I began facilitating what became FaithAgain each month along with ThinkAgain. Initially, I turned to Dan Wotherspoon for ideas for presenters. Dan had been in attendance when Jim spoke and was very supportive. He knew the England family well, having assisted in creating a website to ensure Gene's legacy continued (EugeneEngland.org). Dan's good heart, connections, and talents were helpful, and his contributions to the enduring and growing appreciation for Gene's work have been invaluable.

**THE RECONCILIATION:**

Not too long after that pivotal evening, Jim expressed a desire to meet with Charlotte. Jim had long appreciated Gene's contributions to a more progressive and expansive Latter-day Saint theology. He wanted to offer an apology to her and the England family for how his Uncle Bruce had treated Gene while Gene was a professor at BYU. Many are aware of the controversy over Elder McConkie's public rebuke of Gene for teaching ideas Elder McConkie considered heretical—ideas well within Latter-day Saint theology then and considered fairly mainstream today.

One would need to read the full story of the difficulties between Gene and Elder McConkie—along with McConkie's BYU professor son, Joseph Fielding McConkie—to fully appreciate Gene's exemplary response and to more fully understand the pain, heartache, and professional turmoil it caused him, Charlotte, and their children. Many believe the conflict precipitated Gene eventually being forced to leave BYU. Yet Gene never spoke ill of these two McConkies or attacked them—even as he disagreed with them and was emotionally and materially harmed by them. In the church and in the world, we desperately need to practice such Christian behavior. (A much more complete account of the England-McConkie conflict can be found on the aforementioned website.)

In the spirit of Gene's earlier attempts at reconciliation with the McConkies, and with the hope of helping heal the unresolved discomfort between the two families, Jim asked me to arrange a meeting with Charlotte. Of course, when I reached out to her, she insisted on hosting and serving us dinner. Hosting people for dinner is one of the things Charlotte is famous for. She does it splendidly and graciously, without pretense or show.

It was a summer evening and the late light filtered through Charlotte's windows, giving the dining area a rich warm glow. To be in her lovely home as well as in the presence of her generous mind and spirit was magical. The delicious meal accompanied by her famous chicken, homemade bread, and ice cream made it even more enchanting. Add to that the opportunity to witness these remarkable souls come together while they shared experiences and what each found beautiful and meaningful. Judith, an artist, art historian, and teacher, bonded with Charlotte over their shared love of creating, appreciating, and collecting art.

After dinner, we moved to some nearby chairs. Moving his chair close and directly across from Charlotte, Jim gently shifted attention to the purpose of our gathering. It was deeply moving to see and hear him express with great feeling his love and appreciation for Gene's work and his profound sorrow for what had happened. Jim did not denigrate his uncle but made it clear that Gene deserved much better treatment than he had received.

As much as anyone could adequately apologize for the harm done by a revered relative, Jim did so. Judi also expressed her appreciation for Gene and Charlotte and her sorrow over what the England family had suffered. Eyes glistened with the witness of hearts sharing each other's burdens and with the acknowledgment of wrongs done and the wish to right them—and of being heard, received, and held by a living proxy.

This sacramental sharing of a historical pain was salvific—not just for Charlotte, but also for Jim who had carried the burden of his uncle's actions. Jane and I were grateful to be present for such a grace-filled offering. The sweetness of this poignant, and what I consider a divinely facilitated, moment cannot be adequately conveyed through words.

The following summer, the five of us gathered again, this time at Charlotte and Gene's beautiful rustic cabin up Provo Canyon. Amid the whirring of hummingbirds, the company of turkeys, and the mating calls of peacocks, we shared delicious food, explorations of the heart and mind, and our appreciation for the legacy left by Gene—and Charlotte. I will always live in wonder witnessing these two prominent Latter day Saint families, once in the way with one another, now walking together in reconciliation and friendship. Since that first engagement, our little group of reconcilers has continued to gather and enjoy each other's company.

Several years before his untimely death from brain cancer, Gene wrote the following:

> "Human beings cannot be reduced to an action, a political or intellectual position, a quotation in a newspaper, an essay or a story they have written ... We are never less—and actually much more because of our infinite potential—than the complete sum of our history, our stories, a sum which is constantly increasing, changing, through time." ("On Spectral Evidence," 1993)

These words have never felt more timely, important, and true. May the spirit of Gene's, Charlotte's, Jim's, and Judi's generous hearts live on in our religious, political, and personal interactions.

# Gene England, the Master Teacher

**THOMAS GRIFFITH**

Thomas B. Griffith was a member of the US Court of Appeals for the DC Circuit. He is currently a fellow at the Wheatley Institute at Brigham Young University and a lecturer on law at Harvard Law School.

Like so many others whose lives he touched, shaped, and changed for the better, I first met Gene England through his essays. In March 1975, I was away from BYU on my mission when Gene delivered his speech, "Great Books or True Religion? Defining the Mormon Scholar." A resourceful Honors Program distributed his remarks in pamphlet form, which I read soon after my return to campus. Today, my dog-eared and marginalia-filled copy is wedged tightly between other tattered titles in the "England-ophile" section of my library. From that first encounter with Gene's writing, I read everything I could find that he wrote. I heard in his essays a voice that explained my dearest beliefs, spoke to my deepest concerns, and expressed my highest aspirations. His insights filled my lessons and talks (sometimes with proper attribution). The members of the ward over which I presided must have thought that I was of the view that Gene, along with C.S. Lewis, had been called into the Quorum of the Twelve in a session of general conference they had missed. "Elder G. Eugene England." It fit, right down to the first initial in place of a name.

Because Gene came to BYU only after I had graduated and moved back to the Washington, DC, area, I first met him in person after I had become—unknown to him—his acolyte. It was the winter of 1995. I cashed in my frequent flier miles accumulated with blood, sweat, and tears as a litigation partner at a law firm in DC and took my three oldest children, then in their teens, on a trip to Utah to see the sites, visit BYU, and introduce them to skiing. For the BYU portion of the trip, I allowed each to pick a class to visit. I gave them free reign with one exception. They had to attend with me the class I picked: "Early American Literature," taught by Gene England. There, sitting among thirty or so BYU students in a classroom in the Smith Family Living Center, I introduced my children to the best of BYU. The discussion Gene led that day moved seamlessly from Hawthorne to Alma, back to Hawthorne, on to Paul,

Joseph Smith, and Jeffrey Holland, then back again to Hawthorne. Academic freedom at its best. No artificial distinction between secular and sacred, heart and mind, reason and faith.

I could have left Gene's classroom that day feeling that the purpose of my trip had been achieved. I had shown my children the pursuit of knowledge at its best, by the best. What happened next exceeded my expectations. Gene invited us to meet him in his office to chat. Because his office would have been too small a space even had it not been filled with the clutter of books, papers, and articles, we moved to the faculty lounge. There, for the next hour, Gene directed the conversation not to me but to my teenaged children. He understood what was happening here, what was at stake. Young lives, young hearts, young minds were being shaped and formed. For a great teacher, there are no ordinary moments. And so, I resisted the temptation to ask Gene the hundred questions I had in mind. Instead, I sat back and watched a great teacher talk to my children. I watched him model love, genuine interest, and empathy. At times I had to pinch myself. Here was the man most responsible for the fire of my adult faith and commitment to the church teaching the children I loved more than life, and I knew that he knew what was at stake. It doesn't get any better than that.

Only a few years later, I found myself back at BYU as its general counsel. Gene had moved on to Utah Valley State College (now Utah Valley University), but the acolyte sought out the leader, and there was time to address a few of my hundred questions. The day before he collapsed from what turned out to be the tumor that took him from us, I was in his home talking with Charlotte and Gene about how best to carry out my new responsibilities as a campus stake president. "Emphasize the Savior, speak constantly of the Atonement, and teach that full engagement in the life of the ward is redemptive," he counseled. And I did. And the members of my stake heard much from Gene England (always with proper attribution).

# Religious Thought as Speculative Play

**GEORGE B. HANDLEY**

George B. Handley is professor of interdisciplinary humanities at BYU where he has taught since 1998. A scholar of comparative literature and environmental humanities, he is the author of several books, including most recently *The Hope of Nature: Our Care for God's Creations* and *If Truth Were a Child*. He is also a creative writer and the author of a novel, *American Fork*, and a memoir, *Home Waters*.

The visit of Gene, Charlotte, and their youngest daughters to our home in Connecticut in the early 1980s left an indelible impression. My parents had been trying to help me appreciate the great cultural offerings of New York City for some time, but sometimes it takes a second witness. As the Englands spoke in their inimitable way of museums, the theater, and ballet, I remember wanting to elevate my life and my mind. I remember too that Gene sparked my interest in BYU by flattering me with what I would add if I chose to attend. Graduating seniors from my ward regularly headed out to Utah every year, and the rebel in me said I would do it differently, but he gave me pause. I did apply, but the palm trees of Stanford seduced me, and I left for California.

My freshman year at Stanford was the most stimulating and formative year of my only recently awakened intellectual and spiritual life. In my humanities classes, I was spurred at every turn to define my faith, my philosophy of life, and to give reasons for my opinions on matters small and large, personal and political, philosophical and cosmological. I began to feel the need to find ways to integrate the expanding parts of my young self.

Both the summer before and after my freshman year helped to that end when I worked as a counselor at Lowell Bennion's boys ranch. Lowell, of course, was one of Gene's most important influences, and he quickly became one of mine too. There I enjoyed my first Mormon salon of sorts with my fellow bright-eyed and inquisitive counselors, including for a time Gene's son, Mark. Modeled after the forums Gene had created, we even circulated a few issues of a kind of small-scale *Dialogue*, a newsletter that we created and shared with each other in the mail.

This first taste of Mormon intellectual life drew me to transfer for a semester to BYU before my mission to immerse myself in the world of which Gene had spoken so fondly. Among BYU's greatest hits that I tried out, I and my roommate and fellow counselor, Lindsay Bennion, and Gene's daughter, Becky, took Gene's Mormon literature class, a captivating overview of Mormon fiction, sermons, drama, poetry, and essays. I was persuaded by his argument that Mormons were called to produce great literature and that whatever excellence we would achieve would likely be underappreciated by most members. It felt, nevertheless, that we were studying a tradition that was yet to ripen.

I still have in my possession two essays I wrote for that class. One was a rhetorical analysis of President Kimball's unforgettable speech, "The False Gods We Worship" in 1976 and his second century address to BYU about the glorious potential of Mormon arts and ideas. In those two essays I took to heart both Kimball's extraordinary vision and his ominous warnings about the misuses of my faith. I have reflected often on what an important assignment it was for me to give my critical attention to such speeches by a church leader. It was part of Gene's effort to teach us that the Restored Gospel was resilient and relevant to our time and culture and that it could withstand all scrutiny. I am struck now that Gene was not interested in critiquing or diagnosing why Mormonism hadn't up to that point lived up to such ideals or why other church leaders might have given alternative visions of a Mormon culture. We didn't spend any time examining why the church was promoting subpar visual art, for example, why Deseret Book was publishing pablum, or why young Mormons preferred Afterglow to Bach. What made his class compelling was that he offered a vision of what could be, even if it didn't explain why that new culture was still out of reach.

My second paper was partly an attempt to see if I could get a rise out of Gene, I guess because I found myself resisting some of his apologetics. The existential Christianity in Levi Peterson's short stories had moved me more deeply than anything else we had read that semester. As I read my essay now in all of its sophomoric inadequacy, I think I hoped to make a grand statement about the superiority of fiction in comparison to the personal essay, which he had touted as the quintessential Mormon literary form. The essay was entitled "Taking an Axe to the Chevy, or Why I Like *Canyons of Grace*." We had earlier read his essay "Blessing the Chevrolet," in which he argues for the very practical and secular uses to which priesthood power could be used. I knew he favored provocative titles, so maybe I was trying to imitate him, even as I intended to rib and implicitly critique him. The essay, however, ultimately backed away from arguing directly against the personal essay. Gene didn't flinch in any case, providing generous feedback on the essay and noting only briefly that I never explained the title in the body of the essay.

As a young man with a bit of a chip on my shoulder, I think I felt some ambivalence about what appeared to be his central place as adjudicator of this tradition. On the one hand, no one before or since ever gave me such hope about what kind of literature Mormons could produce, a vision that has never left me. And yet it seemed that all such efforts would inevitably be curated and evaluated by him. I suppose I resented that. I didn't want to play the game of currying his favor, even as I continued to want entrée to the family's inner circle.

The experience of being totally immersed in Mormonism and Mormon culture was exhilarating, so much so that I wavered for the better part of my mission about which school to return to. There was something I had seen happen in Gene's class and in the immersive environment of BYU that happened nowhere else, and yet, there was nothing like the excitement of testing my culture amidst the world's diversity, something BYU could never offer. I am still trying to resolve this dilemma.

Ultimately, I decided to return to Stanford, but I knew that I was going to need to depend, more than ever before, on a Mormon discourse to assist me in the quest for an integrated life. Gene had in the meantime published his collection, *Dialogues with Myself.* I remember not liking the title. Perhaps from my own perceived self-importance as a Stanford student, I felt that Mormon discourse was too narcissistic, too self-obsessed, and I blamed at least part of it on him for seeming to want all of our thought and all of our art to reflect the unique nature of our religious mission. I don't know if my assessment was accurate, but this thought ate at me and kept me away from the symposia of *Dialogue* and *Sunstone.* I was not opposed to them for theological reasons but because I didn't feel drawn to what seemed like too much self-referentiality. As a young man still trying to come to terms with my Mormon identity, I was probably guilty of what he called "provincial anti-provincialism."

Nevertheless, the book was manna in the wilderness. Gene was the only model I had of how to relate the gospel to the pressing questions of our time within the context of the humanities which had become my intellectual home. I wasn't sure I accepted all of his arguments, but they inspired me to want to engage the questions. I remember one of my Stanford professors saw me reading his book, and he asked to borrow it for a few days. He had known Gene at Stanford years before. This was a historian of China, as well as of Western thought, a Jewish atheist gay Marxist who read voraciously and spoke a dozen or more languages. He was the most brilliant mind I had at that point encountered in my life. I worried he would dash the book to pieces and uncover it for the provincial book it was and us for the provincial people we were. He returned it a few days later and praised it for its artistry and intelligence. Alright then. Gene, and maybe Mormonism itself, had passed.

I began my academic career at Northern Arizona, but the BYU seed Gene planted had continued to grow. After three years, in 1998 I applied for a position at BYU, but, when I got the offer, I found myself doubting if I should come. I called Gene, hoping that he would rejoice and convince me to come, but he was sullen and even discouraging. I hadn't been paying much attention to developments on campus or in the world of Mormon intellectualism in general, so I was surprised when he told me not to come. He was in the midst of his tragic departure from BYU, and he simply couldn't promise it would be the land of free intellectual inquiry that he had long claimed it was.

I was torn, but not for the reasons he might have expected. I didn't imagine myself getting into scrums about Mormon culture or Mormon belief. I only wanted to teach my subject of comparative literature. Maybe I would dabble in Mormon things, but I had no ambition to weigh in publicly on every major touchpoint of doctrine that created tension in contemporary contexts. That seemed exhausting and unappealing to me. What worried me more, ironically maybe, was the very idea of an immersive Mormon life that had attracted me to apply. I had tasted of its advantages but could not forget its disadvantages. Nevertheless, I came and immediately began to thrive. Somewhere inside of me I had decided, maybe with a touch of smugness, that I would be less provincial, less self-obsessed, and that I would help expand the horizons of my students and the university accordingly. I regret that I wasn't more sympathetic to what was happening to Gene. The excitement of my own horizons overshadowed the collapse of his significant contributions to my faith community and to BYU.

Moreover, it would take me years to realize that, despite significant and much-needed gains in scholarly excellence, we ended up paying a cost for pivoting as an institution this way. The Gene England style of thought was out and academic professionalism and peer-reviewed scholarship in our fields was in. Provincial anti-provincialism was not uncommon and, as a result, doctrines of the church and ideas of the world were taught, but they seemingly rarely met. This made it increasingly difficult for students to navigate contemporary culture because it forced false choices between fidelity to the gospel or fidelity to secular ideas, something I felt in my very bones was false and harmful to the church and to secular culture alike. The church called for more integration of faith and learning to help our students, but many faculty felt that you risked getting punished like Gene if you made the effort, or the result might just be mediocrity. Encouragements to the contrary, the church seemed to prefer the less messy option of keeping the sacred and secular compartmentalized.

Integration of faith and intellect takes a lot of work and thought and requires experimentation. This means patience with the poor thinking that can result, a patience that is hard to come by in our age of increased polarization. Excessive dogmatism leads to insufficient integration and to premature and erroneous conclusions in religious thought, but when religious thought is embraced as a form of speculative play, it might generate mistakes, but it is also more likely to achieve greatness. Gene had more of the latter than the former, but one thing for sure is that he was the most tirelessly at play, and as he often reminded his students, as Hugh B. Brown once said, the only cure for bad thinking was more thinking.

Perhaps a greater tragedy is not that the institution let him down—which seems obvious—or that he made some intellectual mistakes in his own thinking or writing—which seems inevitable for any writer of ambition. It is perhaps that the range and diversity of voices engaging in such thinking were so limited. The church is right to expect faithful scholarship from BYU faculty, but in my experience the paucity of such work isn't caused by lack of testimony but by an atmosphere of insufficient trust. It seems that as a church community, we haven't overcome a persistent ambivalence toward the kind of faithful scholarship we say we want. For every sign of progress—a thriving and more diverse community of faithful scholars at BYU and throughout the church that I am privileged to be a part of—in-fighting, turf wars, institutional whiplash, and suspicion continue apace.

Both my professor at Stanford and Gene both have long since passed away. Reflecting on Gene's legacy, I find myself wondering how my efforts might measure up to the high and different expectations alike that these two professors and their respective institutions represent. I am not sure, but I at least can attest to two things: BYU has given me generous support to thrive as a scholar of postcolonial literature, and its unique and stimulating religious environment has facilitated my ventures into that unique heritage Gene first taught me that I was fortunate to have as a member of the church. I can only hope for enough forbearance and trust for me to eventually get it right.

# A Mentor for Dissent and Devotion at BYU

**MAXINE HANKS**

Maxine Hanks is a historian and theologian specializing in women's studies in religion. She took her bachelor's degree in gender studies from the University of Utah and completed graduate work in history at ASU and theology at Harvard Divinity School. She has authored, coauthored, and edited a number of books and published numerous articles, essays, and web media on Mormonism and other subjects. She was one of the "September Six" Latter-day Saints excommunicated in 1993, then served in interfaith ministry for thirteen years before returning to the LDS Church in 2012, where she currently serves as a Sunday school teacher.

In the spring of 1980, I arrived in Provo as a returned missionary trying to find myself. All my Mormon friends had moved to Utah for school, but I dreaded attending the Y, which seemed steeped in marriage making. I needed something more mentally stimulating than dating. I longed to study philosophy at Harvard, but my working-class background offered no support for higher education. I found myself driving to Provo, with no place else to go, and turning to the few students I knew—my former missionary companions.

That was how I wound up at the home of Gene and Charlotte England. One of my mission sisters was living in the basement of the Englands' stately brick residence at 1775 Andrus Lane. The address itself evoked notions of freedom and independence.

I descended the stairs to find my friend, Ginger, and her roommate, Jody England, seeming relaxed and refreshingly authentic. We chatted about school and missions, deferring marriage until graduation, and classes that led to actual careers. I sensed that I had stumbled onto the cognoscenti: the England enclave was my entre to a scholarly subculture, a world where uncommon views were welcome.

Ginger told me about Jody's father, Eugene England, a professor with progressive ideas and pursuits. He was affiliated with a scholarly publication, like the ones at Ivy League schools, called *Dialogue: A Journal of Mormon Thought*. Created in 1966 by Gene and some friends when they were attending Stanford University, *Dialogue* offered an array of religious and intellectual ideas that I wasn't finding at Deseret Book. I couldn't believe my luck—I'd found a Stanford scholar at BYU.

Gene was a role model, like an academic parent for students striving to think and write in probing and erudite ways. He introduced us to liberal ideas, complex narratives, scholarly critiques, and humanitarian causes. He valued freedom of speech, deep analysis, and ethical dissent, along with devotion to divine truth, spiritual principles, and higher wisdom.

We were inspired by Gene and *Dialogue*, so we students started our own liberal independent publication at BYU in 1981—called the *Seventh East Press*. Gene would drop by our office now and then to deliver manuscripts and watch us in action, always lending his support. Whenever he appeared in our spartan upper room above Kinkos Copies and Grandpa's Used Books, we felt graced by celebrity. He smiled in sympathy, remembering his own student days at Stanford, and wistfully reminisced, "Ah, youth!" We felt legitimized by his sincere interest in our efforts.

We admired Gene's commitment to academic inquiry coupled with his abiding faith, intellectual honesty, and inner spirituality. He was devoted to both his church community and humanitarian causes, like Food for Poland. He organized a campaign to feed starving workers striking behind the Iron Curtain, led by Lech Walesa and his Solidarity movement. I interviewed Gene to write about Food for Poland in our paper, while the England family and volunteers worked around the clock to gather food for strangers, half a world away.

When Apostle Bruce R. McConkie privately chastised Gene for sharing personal views about eternal progression, we were given a copy of McConkie's letter circulating underground. We debated whether or not to publish it. We wanted to expose what we believed was ecclesiastical intimidation of an exemplary and ethical professor. Yet, I nixed our making it public out of respect for Gene's privacy. In 1983, BYU banned the *Seventh East Press* from campus for printing controversial topics, which ended the paper. Gene felt bad about it, yet he understood the price of dissent, and he sympathized with our plight.

After that, I was hired by the College of Humanities as a manuscript editor, assisting BYU professors with their articles and essays for publication. I found myself editing faculty whom I'd admired as a student and reporter—a rather intimidating task. However, the insights I'd learned from Gene helped me to support his colleagues in conveying their faith and scholarship. As a young editor, I learned from Gene (along with Linda Adams and Arthur Henry King) the exquisite gifts of perfecting prose via rhetorical skills of poetics, grammar, and style, and how to balance scholarly and personal voice, and argument and inspiration. Gene and Arthur taught me precision and grace of expression and helped me smooth the rough edges of my working-class dialect and relax my feminist defensiveness.

My office was down the hall from Gene's, which was an oasis of open thought and honest questions. I tried to emulate his safe haven for students. I started a club for peace and human rights, and asked Gene to be its advisor. Always willing to mentor progressive efforts, he named the club "Response" to inspire dialogue between students and faculty. We sponsored symposia with faculty speakers like Gene, Mike Quinn, Tom Rogers, and Alan Keele, and outside activists like Will Whittle, Helen Caldicott, and journalist Sydney Schanberg (who helped Dith Pran escape from communist Cambodia).

Eventually, we former students and *Press* staff members moved to Salt Lake where we continued our engagement of dissent and devotion by writing and editing for *Sunstone* and Signature Books. We found ourselves speaking alongside Gene at Mormon studies conferences in the late 1980s and early 1990s. When Gene and I shared a panel on Mormon theology at Sunstone in 1990, I was shaking in my shoes, but Gene defended my feminist perspective by ameliorating the criticisms aimed at me. While panelists battled, Gene's calming voice rose above the din and settled the polarization like a dove descending. He always made seemingly irreconcilable ideas sensible and conciliatory.

As a middle kid and misfit, my innate tendency was to land and mediate between opposing views. In Gene, I saw a gifted, fully mature, empowered version of the peacemaker. His calm demeanor and conciliatory mind made the role of mediating real for me. The precedent he set made it safer for me to inhabit the paradoxical middle ground.

When several scholars, feminists, and BYU faculty were disciplined, fired, or excommunicated in 1993, Gene was deeply concerned and empathetic, offering solace and solidarity for our freedom of conscience. He publicly refuted the church denouncement of scholarly symposia and the silencing of BYU professors' public views. He voiced the unavoidable dilemma, our common conundrum, the paradox that plagued us all—the tension between dissent and devotion. There was no escape: each of us had to navigate his or her own way.

When Gene was forced to leave BYU in 1998 in order to pursue his freedom to explore that elusive balance between devotion and dissent, he was part of the larger "purge of the 1990s." His dismissal echoed our own exile in 1993. Yet, at UVU Gene created one of the earliest university Mormon studies programs, pioneering safety and support for mature scholarly engagement of LDS religion. His program heartened hope, and defended the work of many who had lost their positions or memberships—a crucial effort at that time.

Gene never ceased pursuing his ideals of dialogue, mutual understanding, common ground, and truth "made manifest by proving contraries," as Joseph

Smith prescribed. Gene was committed to marrying his conscience with faith, merging his quest for social justice with spiritual ideals, and mentoring young minds in Utah County (and beyond) with spirit and intelligence, light and truth.

Gene was a beacon of balance amid the endless tensions of devotion versus dissent. He embodied the life of the mind, heart, and soul, working together as one. His was a life well lived. His light still radiates in his writings, in his family, and in the minds of countless students, associates, and friends.

In my memory, he abides as a cherished mentor. I'm still engaging the deeper dialogues, principled responses, and mediating ways he taught me, as I continue to write and speak today.

# Walking Hope

**SUSAN M. HINCKLEY**

Susan Hinckley is a storyteller in words and pictures. Her widely published and exhibited art is held in private collections across the US. She has reflected on her faith and church experiences in books, in *Exponent II*, *Sunstone*, and *Dialogue*, and as co-creator of the *At Last She Said It* podcast.

I lived with a lot of anxiety as a child, and that anxiety latched onto church as often as anything. So much was handed to me as "truth" that the most trivial things were weighty by association. I had a hard time untangling what was really important from what was not. So, I worried about all of it.

I worried about getting water up my nose at my baptism. Also, about the problem of remaining perfect. How long could it be before I messed it all up? By age eight, I knew enough from watching grownups to understand perfection was a losing proposition.

I worried about the moon turning to blood, a fear planted in my overactive mind by a young returned missionary called to sub in Sunday school at the last minute. He thought eschatological horror stories would be the perfect thing to hold the attention of impressionable ten-year-olds. It worked too well.

I worried about polygamy. I knew it had been done away with, but I couldn't ever wrap my heart around it being God's idea to begin with. What would keep a God who wasn't too concerned about being fair to girls from bringing it back?

Before I was even clear on the details of how babies were born, I worried about having to give birth to eternities of them. By junior high, I worried about the stirrings of ambition I felt in myself that had nothing to do with babies. Did good Mormon girls want to run away to design school? Could they become geologists?

I worried about things as big as exaltation and as small as taking the sacrament with my right hand. Could there really be a connection between the two? By the time I finished high school, I had worried about it all so much, I associated little if any peace with anything related to church.

As a young adult, the temple tightened the grip of my anxiety. Why was

I troubled by the promises demanded of me? What if I didn't put my temple clothes on in the right order? What if I couldn't remember the answers when asked to repeat them? What if I needed to leave? Did being so miserable with worry mean I didn't belong in his holy house?

In my married church life, I worried about how much I still chafed under the leadership and supervision of men. Would I ever not feel rebellious when a man told me what I must do or how I must do it? Would my heart ever not pound when someone in a suit and tie asked me to step into his office to receive a calling? Must I always accept, even if I cried with dread all the way home?

My worries matured with me. I began to realize I would probably never control my unruly thoughts. I didn't agree with things I heard in talks and lessons at church, or couldn't make logical sense of them. Even as an adult, I perceived no space to ask the questions of my heart or express my struggle to believe.

I worried about being discovered as an imposter—losing the life I was building, the life I was sacrificing for, and the life I loved—if I couldn't toe the line. Did other members have these feelings? I worried they did not.

As my daughters grew, I worried about raising them to become healthy women in the confines of a church I'd never figured out how to be a happy woman in myself. I worried about losing them. If I couldn't control their choices in this life, must I resign myself to being separated in the next?

I yearned to hear, "We don't really know what the next life will be like, so there's not much use worrying about it. Instead, work on loving this life." No one at church said that. But if I wasn't meant to focus on this world, why did I love it so much? How could I see things so differently? I blamed myself, but couldn't help blaming God a little too, for telling me one thing while he told others something else.

Most members with whom I interacted didn't seem bothered by any of this. Was I just determined to miss the point? Still, I couldn't imagine leaving the church. Even after a lifetime of uneasiness and uncertainty there, with all my heart I just wanted the peace I'd been promised.

Which brings me to Eugene England. When I received his essay, "Why the Church is as True as the Gospel," it felt like someone quietly slipping a lifeline into my grasping spiritual hands. A friend sent it to me in the mail, saying, "Here is something I think might help you." That's all.

There had been scriptures through the years that had comforted me, and words from leaders and teachers along the way to which I had pinned my hope. But I first glimpsed a possibility larger than all my worried questions in the suggestion that salvation might lie in my response to the "other, exasperating Saints" with whom I'd spent my life struggling. How my friend knew the message I'd been waiting to hear, I don't know. Just as Eugene England will never know his part in my story, she'll never understand the gift she gave by introducing me to his words. He wrote hope for me.

In the essay he mentions Joseph Smith's assertion that "by proving contraries, truth is made manifest." England goes on to explain, "By 'prove' he meant not only to demonstrate logically but to test, to struggle with, and to work out in practical experience. The church is as true—as effective—as the gospel because it involves us directly in proving contraries, working constructively with the oppositions within ourselves and especially between people, struggling with paradoxes and polarities at an experiential level that can redeem us. The church is true because it is concrete, not theoretical; in all its contradictions and problems, it is at least as productive of good as is the gospel."

In these words, I began to understand that even my contrariness might be made holy. I saw the possible sanctification of a lifetime of worries. These things made me who I was, but they didn't dictate who I became next. I saw a prescription to alleviate my anxiety with action, worry redeemed by reframing the wrestle as spiritual work, letting it grow me rather than keep me small and afraid. I could be—indeed had already been—made better through my willingness to keep walking among the Saints, even when the walk was always uphill.

I also caught a first glimpse of a spiritual gift within myself. Struggling at church had equipped me with a specific kind of empathy, a lifeline I could offer others that not all members had. No matter how worried my steps, the movement of my feet on the ground had actually always been a manifestation of my faith. Needing to work hard for a thing didn't mean I wasn't worthy of it. By reframing the church's purpose in my life, I could claim peace for myself, right where I was standing.

I've found peace in many of Eugene England's words in the years since that first encounter with an essay offered me a place to rest, reset, and refocus. I pick up that original lifeline and read it again, whenever I need to feel hope made tangible in my hands. But one of my favorite lines will always be, "I believe that any good church is a school of love . . ." I believe that too. In all my struggle to understand, and all my worry about doing things right or getting them wrong, I hadn't considered making love the focus of my church life. In wrestling its shadows, I'd missed embracing the real thing.

The suggestion that working to see others the way God sees them might be the first step in my own salvation—a salvation here and now, in which I finally have a better understanding of the way God sees me—shifted my focus from reward to spiritual growth, reframing the church as a workshop rather than a source of worry. The sure words of this man, acknowledging opposition while explaining how love might turn it into something that pulls me forward, continue to inform my steps. "I know God has been found by unusual people in unusual places," he wrote. He's right. I've found God in myself, and in the church too—places I'd failed to reliably find him before.

# God's Spy

## CLIFTON H. JOLLEY

Clifton Jolley has published in *Western Folklore Quarterly*, the *New York Times*, *Deseret News*, the *Salt Lake Tribune*, *Ensign*, *Music and the Spoken Word*, KUED's *Civic Dialogue*, and elsewhere. His documentaries have been broadcast nationally by PBS. He began writing personal essays because Gene England told him it is "the Mormon genre."

> Human beings cannot be reduced to an action, a political or intellectual position, a quotation … an essay or a story they have written … We are never less—and actually much more because of our infinite potential—than the complete sum of our history, our stories, a sum which is constantly increasing, changing, through time. —G. Eugene England ("On Spectral Evidence")

In a 2021 issue of *Meridian Magazine*, an article asks a question: "Have You Heard this Myth about Hugh B. Brown?" That title is the only question the article asks, presuming to know better the meaning of a remark Elder Brown made at a 1969 BYU assembly: "An Eternal Quest—Freedom of the Mind."

Early in his devotional presentation, Elder Brown said, "We are not so much concerned with whether your thoughts are orthodox or heterodox as we are that you shall have thoughts."

Mormon liberals consider this an important statement encouraging individual thought and testimony and even the expression of what may be considered *heterodoxic* opinions and insights. The *Meridian* authors call such an understanding "myth." Setting aside the clear intention of the title—freedom of thought in the context of religious experience (which Elder Brown addressed on several occasions)—the authors argue that Elder Brown is endorsing only the sort of freedom that arrives at the conclusions *they* interpret to be orthodox.

Clearly, Elder Brown anticipates that free enquiry can lead to true testimony, but he does not dismiss the importance of "freedom of the mind," wherever it leads:

> You young people live in an age when freedom of the mind is superseded and suppressed over much of the world. We must preserve it in the Church and in America and resist all efforts of earnest men to suppress it … Preserve, then, the

freedom of your mind in education and in religion and be unafraid to express your thoughts and to insist upon your right to examine every proposition.

Gene would have less argument with many in the church had he not so deeply believed in this principle of *enquiry* and *dialogue* between good people seeking a common goal: Truth. Not *a* truth we entirely understand, but as we are increasingly coming to understand it and continue to seek an understanding that is intended by God ever to be evolving.

Six months before he was compelled to retire from Brigham Young University, Gene delivered an address to the BYU English Department in which he gave a confounding definition of what he believed is required of a Latter-day Saint academic: to be at once faithful to revealed doctrine as well as informed by the investigative methodologies of the higher criticism espoused by new critics such as Wayne Booth (who was moved—by attending one of Gene's Sunday school lessons—not to have his name removed from the records of the church).

In an essay made all the more tragic by its publication after his death—"No Cause, No Cause: An Essay Toward Reconciliation"—Gene quotes Elder Marion D. Hanks as stating that "if the gospel were not true, he would want to be the first to know, and so he must always be willing to look at all the evidence." This Gene discerned to be a moment of "conservative confidence and liberal openness," which suggests a baseline for what he regarded in Mormonism as true conservativism (confidence/testimony) and true liberalism (openness/investigation). At the very least, it defines why he considered himself to be both a conservative and a liberal, providing a path perhaps more available to liberals than to conservatives, but unlikely to satisfy either.

This ambiguity of purposes and outcomes Gene attributes to a kind of inevitable tragedy, as evidenced by his title's source material: *King Lear* (Act 5, Scene 3), in which Lear pleads with his youngest daughter, Cordelia, hoping for a remedy in proportion to the damage he has done:

"If you have poison for me, I will drink it ..."

Lear assures his faithful daughter (whom he has misjudged and grievously wronged):

"You have some cause ..."

To which she replies,

"No cause, no cause."

Which gives Gene his title, and his theme: *No cause for recrimination by those who have been wronged. All cause for reconciliation with those who have been wrong.*

But Gene's introduction to the essay makes inevitable the defeat of any reconciliation he may have hoped for, especially if that hope depended on Saints who believe that "follow the Prophet" means a mindless, unquestioning servitude to an all-encompassing ecclesiastical "authority" that should govern our religious beliefs and day-to-day lives.

In the introduction, Gene recounts two "profound spiritual experiences" he describes as "more like encounters" that resulted in him becoming "both a conservative and a liberal and both orthodox and unorthodox." In other words—and regardless of his lifelong effort to persuade those who are unpersuadable—Gene would wind up offending someone somewhere much (if not most) of the time. And toward the end of his life, he evidently made peace with the fact that he was not strictly the "conservative" with whom retrograde conservatives ever would make peace.

Nor, I think, was his "liberalism" simply that expression of beneficence described by Bob Rees in his thoughtful and moving memorial essay "Reimagining the Restoration: Why Liberalism is the Ultimate Flowering of Mormonism." Although Bob's essay is wise and descriptive of Gene's generosity of spirit and his lifelong effort to be obedient to conflicting obligations of faith, conscience, and affiliation, it may work too hard to associate "liberalism" with liberals (although it takes a few good swings at them too). Perhaps the more important aspect of Gene's *liberalism* was the *conservatism* from which it sprang: a farm kid's consecration by his earthly father to the service of his Heavenly Father—which consecration created an even greater conundrum for Gene's father than it appeared to for Gene. As his father told me of the son he had promised to God's service and the trouble it had caused (and would cause) church administrators: "Look at what they do to my son!"

This disconnect between the *calling* and the *service* was anticipated by Elder B. H. Roberts, as noted by Bob Rees in his essay:

> Roberts distinguished between what he calls "disciples pure and simple … whose whole intellectual life … consists of their partisanship … and mere repetition" of religious formulas and those disciples who "bring to the new teaching, from the first, their own personal contribution … [and] help lead the thought that they accept to a truer expression. They force it beyond its earlier and cruder stages of development." Note his use of the word "force," which in this context I think Roberts intended "[to] bring about by unusual effort." Roberts added, and this is the part of his essay most relevant to reimagining the Restoration, that Mormonism "calls for thoughtful disciples who will not be content with merely repeating some of its truths, but will develop its truths; and enlarge … [Mormonism] by that development."

But while Gene would have agreed with Bob's parsing of the term "force," it's clear that Gene's intention to *bring about by unusual effort* was not similarly forgiven by apostles more modern than Roberts.

And Gene was aware that quoting B. H. Roberts or Marion D. Hanks or Hugh B. Brown does not dismiss the sterner, less adventuresome, and more punishing voices of the stricter *conservatives* among the Brethren. And he discovered that his pacifism did not—as was the case with the Anti-Nephi-Lehies—soften the hearts of those conservatives who viewed him as an undisciplined interloper on a field of enquiry less ideal than described by John Milton, who stated in *Areopagitica*:

> Give me the liberty to know, to utter, and to argue freely according to conscience, above all liberties.

But it is clear that many of those who considered Gene "argumentative" believed their calling permitted *only them* the liberty to wield the sword of correct thinking. Nor was Gene willing to take up a sword that wounded the leadership of the church, some of whom desired to exchange sagacity for complicity, who appeared to think striving for agreement is little more than puerile appeasement.

Gene spent his life struggling to arrive at a definition of *liberal belief* acceptable to "conservatives," and to resolve his *orthodox* scholasticism with what many church leaders parsed as his *unorthodox* faith. All the while his own conservatism was evident in his confidence in the Gospel of Jesus Christ as revealed through the Prophet Joseph Smith and sustained by the subsequent oracles of Mormonism … all of whom he supported as prophets, seers, and revelators; some of whom he agreed with much of the time while disagreeing with them at least some of the time.

Many with whom he disagreed more of the time—or, more significantly, who disagreed with him—did not see his many essays and contemplations as striving toward a gospel understanding, but as rebellion, which unjust allegation of rebellion worked for those authorities more conspiratorial in their view of the world, and of Gene.

Similarly, many of us who loved and respected Gene may also tend to interpret him to be saying and being what *we want him to be*, whether hero of the liberals—who at the moment have little ecclesiastical power in our culture—or the villain of conservatives, who begin by being suspicious of academics and conclude by seeing in Gene a conspiracy rather than a conversation.

If we are Mormons wracked by the enquiry, indecision, and apparent doubt fundamental to liberal scholasticism, and if despite our doubts we continue to wonder about a God so apparently difficult to discern, then Gene is a liberal (more or less).

If we are Latter-day Saints interested more in what the modern prophets dictate than what the ancient prophets worried over, then Gene—for his constant effort to reach peaceful settlements with those authorities who disagreed with him—is a conservative (more or less).

If we are charismatics more committed to the spiritual experience than the intellectual travail, the "encounters" of Gene's youth—spiritual experiences that would shape his faith and trust in the gospel to the very end of his life—may yet inspire us not to be discouraged by the fact that there still are Korihors among us who seek to trivialize spiritual experiences not their own.

But whether or not he was everything others believe him to have been, any definition must include Gene's own of the "ideal Mormon scholar," who is:

> … critical and innovative as his gifts from God require but conscious of and loyal to his own unique heritage and nurturing community and thus able to exercise those gifts without harm to others or himself.

Shortly before he died, I visited Gene in the hospital where cysts and part of a tumor had been removed from his brain (an affliction all the more tragic since it was one of the great brains among the people and religion he loved). As I leaned over to greet and kiss him, he grabbed me by the collar and pulled me still closer to whisper: "I've had the miracle." At the time, I thought he meant the miracle of healing his life-threatening disease. But, of course, he wasn't healed. At least, not in the way I understood him to mean.

But since I am like everyone who either loves or loathes George Eugene England—seeking to understand him in terms that make the most sense to me—I am now inclined to hope that those last words to me were a summary, a benediction on all that he had tried and everything he had hoped. And perhaps a reconciliation with *the miracle* that much of what he had tried, he had failed to accomplish; especially in terms of reconciling the truths he had discovered (or had been given) with the rage of those who disagreed with and persecuted him—those who, for the most part, did not mend their manners or their visions of a mission they believed to be in opposition to his own—opposition which deprived Gene of consistently being that *happy warrior* he so much of the time appeared to be, his liberal intellect and scholasticism causing conflict with those who shared his conservative testimony but not his liberal pursuit of truth, wherever it may lead. As a result, the peace he most often found was that promised by Jesus:

> … not as the world giveth, give I [peace] unto you. (John 14:27 KJV)

And it's conceivable that toward the end of his mortality, the unruly divine peace promised by Jesus gave Gene less comfort in *the good fight* than he had when he was younger and believed it possible for the revelation of Mormonism to seek further truths and understandings, to evolve. He understood that without evolution—especially beyond the mistakes of practice and doctrine familiar to our past (and, in increasingly difficult and dangerous ways, to our present)—we cannot remain true to the original revelations of Mormonism.

But if his vision was disappointed—of a church forever growing nearer to truths we cannot anticipate but must strive to achieve—he did not fail in his father's consecration or God's invitation. Rather, he accepted Lear's encouragement of Cordelia to "take upon the mystery of things."

Things Gene described as "encounters" so clear and compelling that—regardless of opposition by whatever rank or authority short of God's own command—he would not betray, however difficult the calling, however disappointing the outcomes, however complex his twin devotions to liberalism and conservatism. What his fathers (earthly and heavenly) consecrated and invited him to become, he became ... however dangerous that becoming seemed to those who thought him not a collaborator but a detractor. He wanted to be the one, never intended to be the other, but was what Lear described to Cordelia as one of:

> ... God's spies: and we'll wear out,
> In a wall'd prison, packs and sects of great ones,
> That ebb and flow by the moon.

The "prison" which ever threatened Gene was symbolic, as Shakespeare intended for us to interpret the conclusion of Lear's life, his catharsis, and the failure of his final dream to enjoy his rediscovery of Cordelia, his youngest, most faithful, most Christlike daughter ... who was soon to be hanged.

Perhaps the fate of all visionaries is to anticipate more than they can accomplish. And I do not expect to discover whether Gene's efforts to enlarge upon our understanding of our faith—a faith that began on an Upstate New York farm, although its mission and our understanding of it were never intended by God to stay there, whether geographically, theologically, or theocratically—will continue to encourage us to extend ourselves into the future to which Joseph Smith and Gene England instructed us to seek. Which is where we will find them both, near that "sea of glass" where we need not be conservatives or liberals, but may finally know that truth Gene was seeking.

But until that day:

> The weight of this sad time we must obey,
> Speak what we feel, not what we ought to say ...

# Eugene England: A Personal Memory

**CHAD JONES**

Chad K. Jones is a retired director of corporate communication for Questar Corporation. He lives near half of his twenty grandchildren in southern Utah with his wife, Deb, his book collection, and his mountain bike.

It would be a safe bet that Lech Walesa has been mentioned only once in the 160-odd-year history of Heber City sacrament meetings. But one snowy November morning, that's what the Heber 4th Ward got: Walesa (and Poland's plight) woven into anecdotes about Lowell Bennion, Hugh Nibley, and LeGrand Richards. It was classic Eugene England, and I was in heaven.

In 1985, my faith was flagging. It wasn't doctrine or history that prompted what we now call a faith crisis, but a philosophical alienation from my community. My journal describes what happened next:

> Then the best thing that could have happened did. I went to work for a kindred spirit. They were few and far between, but there he was. In our first few weeks together, I expressed frustration at being out of step (with fellow members). (My new boss) pointed me to Richard Poll's essay "What the Church Means to People Like Me," and a new book, *Why the Church is as True as the Gospel* by Eugene England. I have never been the same since. The tone and spirit of their essays hit home, but more importantly, they helped me realize I was part of a community. It was an admittedly small community, but, hey, I grew up in the minority. If I was going to suffer the slings and arrows of living on the fringe, I had better decide it was worth it—at the very least, decide if it was the best path for me. It was gratifying to know there were others out there who had asked and were still asking the tough questions and had decided it was more than worth it.

My half-empty cup became half-full after reading Gene's essay, "On Finding Truth and God."

By 1990, I was a young bishop's counselor trying to find sacrament-meeting speakers. I thought it would be nearly impossible to get the man who had helped restore my faith to come to Heber. To my mind, it would be like asking Billy Joel to perform at my birthday. But I should have known better. With trepidation, I called Gene who instantly agreed, but suggested I clear it with our bishop. My bishop trusted me, and the Heber 4th Ward heard some of its best sermons ever from Eugene and Charlotte.

I met the Englands in the foyer after they had braved a Provo Canyon snowstorm and ushered them into the bishop's office for a quick pre-meeting prayer. I mentioned that the essays in his book, Richard Poll's *History and Faith* and Philip Barlow's *A Thoughtful Faith*, had sustained me through five tough years as a "Liahona" among "Iron Rods." He smiled without comment.

It was a less fussy era, and so I recorded the Englands' talks. Over the years, I've listened to the cassette, then CD, and now audio file, when traveling on Sundays. Re-listening to Gene's sermon throughout my thirty-five-year career in corporate communication, I realized that Gene, while sharing an important message, had also taught a master class in "knowing your audience." Our congregation was very conservative, rural, middle-class—the salt of the Mormon earth. Few had heard of *Dialogue*, BYU's faculty wars, or Sunstone symposia. None, myself included, were even remotely aware that McConkie's famous "Seven Deadly Heresies" had anything to do with Gene.

It was the holiday season, so Gene laid out the qualifications for being able to hear herald angels. The criteria: promoting peace and charity—two subjects that could easily tip into "pacifism and welfare," the advocacy of which would instantly alienate many listeners.

Gene used folksy humor to subtly establish his bona fides as a small-town boy with scholarly credentials. He critiqued his own actions instead of indicting others, while referencing scripture and official statements. He displayed real emotion—choking up while reminding us "vengeance is (God's)." As he prepared to wrap up, Gene softened the audience for some very pointed challenges by name-dropping the venerated Hugh Nibley (a name the audience would recognize), marveling at how "remarkably outspoken" Nibley was on pacifism and environmentalism. Then, in classic Gene England style, he quickly wrapped up his remarks in his own remarkably outspoken way by quoting Alma, King Benjamin, and Christ.

Although he never indicated such, I felt Gene was also speaking directly to me. I believe he had discerned from our bishop's-office discussion the kind of message I needed to hear to feel a part of my community. Afterward, he asked me if it was OK in a way that seemed like he was asking if I was OK.

About six years after Gene's death, I thought the England family ought to have copies of the recordings and so wrote a note explaining what Gene's writing and life's example meant to me and sent it to Charlotte at the famous England house in Provo. She was graceful and grateful and mentioned she was gathering material for a biography. I never expected to hear from her again. Then, last year, Charlotte called our home to thank my wife and me again and let us know we'd be receiving copies of his biographies as a gift.

When told we had already purchased them, she offered to send them to our son instead.

Terryl Givens's and Kristine Haglund's biographies are both great—deep, philosophical, academic, and full of history, religion, and interesting personal details. And I've been pleasantly pleased to see acknowledgement of what is obvious to those who respected Gene—how his valiant stands on everything from grace to race are working their way into our regular discourse and doctrine.

More important to me, however, was the Christian example I saw in that very short hour in Heber City with Gene and Charlotte. Their charitably showing up for a younger unknown brother and teaching the gospel by word and deed was all the evidence I needed to know that the church is as true as the gospel.

# Eugene England: Gatekeeper to Heaven

**LORRAINE BRADFORD KELLEY**

Before succumbing in 2020 to a 2003 breast cancer diagnosis, Lorraine Bradford Kelley lived a socially, spiritually, and physically energetic fifty-nine-year life with scores of friends and family, attributable in large part to her unconditionally loving acceptance and enjoyment of others, no matter how similar or different from her. She received degrees in the humanities from the University of Maryland and in modern dance from UC–Irvine, served a full-time mission in the Philippines, taught classes to students in her areas of expertise, and mentored many others. Her greatest loves were (and continue to be) her husband, David E. Kelley, and their combined family of seven children and an ever-growing number of grandchildren.

As a teenager, I focused on gymnastics, dance, and social life. Although I valued my religion and family, they were not my priority. Schoolwork was also not a priority. I did not consider myself an intellectual or even a good student.

My parents both had advanced degrees; my dad had a PhD in economics and my mom an MA in English. They valued education almost as highly as family and religion. My brothers were both good students. Scott, my younger brother, was a genius and excelled in every subject. In his freshman year of high school, he was taking twelfth- grade AP math. Steve was on the honor rolls, took AP classes, and received academic recognition. I was proud of my brothers for their intellectual accomplishments, but at times I felt like the black sheep of the family. While Steve and Scott were receiving academic awards, I was nominated by my senior class for the "Air Head" and "Best Looking" awards. Fortunately, I didn't win either.

At BYU in my freshman year, I was interested in getting an education and a degree, but I was also apprehensive. I was creative. I loved to dance, and I loved people. But I didn't know who I really was and what I wanted to do with my life.

My mother and her professor friends from BYU encouraged me to take their honors classes. I declined, thinking I wasn't smart enough. I did, however, take Eugene England's freshman English class. Suddenly, a world of knowledge opened up for me. I was no longer studying just to get into college, or just to please my parents. I was thrilled to be in Eugene's class just for the sake of learning. Fascinated by literature, I realized that people didn't have to choose between art, religion, or education but could choose all of those things.

In my sophomore year, I broke down and took Eugene England's honors class, along with honors science. Brother England taught us that art, religion, science, and literature are interrelated. We as students were becoming philosophers. He taught us to think. He inspired us to delve into the contradictions and the truths.

When my brother, Steve, came back from his mission, we lived next door to each other and became close friends. We shared a mutual social life for the first time, including doing things with the England family. Steve and I, as well as Scott, the next year, spent numerous days at the Englands' house having dinner, discussing school and religion, and getting all the tender loving care we missed living so far from home. This was our home away from home with another brother and five additional sisters.

One day on the way to class, I was in a car accident that left me with severe whiplash and some emotional trauma. The Englands let me stay with them for three weeks while they nursed me back to health. They took turns bringing me food, talking to me about school, helping me with homework, and entertaining me with their humor and love.

Steve, Scott and I loved to visit the Englands' cabin and Ray and Caroline Hillam's cabin with other student friends of ours. We went to commune with nature and to explore our doubts and beliefs. We had enlightened conversations while sitting on the mountaintop enjoying all of God's creations. These discussions were inspired mostly by Eugene's classes.

Brother England, as we called him then, was not predictable. I often had differing views from others around me and sometimes was a little bit proud and stubborn in my "radical" ideas. It surprised me when the liberal Gene played devil's advocate just when I thought he was going to agree with everything I had to say. At first I was disappointed, but I soon became fascinated by his ability to help me see differing views. He helped teach me tolerance of the "Molly/Joe Mormons," as well as to gain greater appreciation for the "intellectuals," all the while inspiring me to write, act, dance, and be myself—no labels at all.

In my second semester sophomore year, I joined the Englands and other BYU students for a semester abroad in London, England. Brother England taught British literature and creative writing. Brother Monroe Paxman taught British history, and Brother Don Marshall taught humanities and the arts. Dashing across London at the last minute to see the latest Broadway show, opera, ballet, or symphony, we had VIP front-row seats. Brother England wanted us to experience everything. With our teachers we explored theatre, dance, history, poetry, architecture, music, paintings, and sculptures.

While studying in London, we traveled by train across Europe for a month. We also spent a week with families in Ireland, and a week each in Russia and Israel. These trips taught me more than I learned during the rest of my college career. Not only was this experience culturally mind-opening, but because of Brother England, it was also a spiritual awakening. He taught us how religion had inspired the arts. We visited gorgeous churches of varying faiths. We felt a fierce connection to God.

When in Russia, I came down with the flu, sick and nervous, so far from home. Brother England missed an important event to bring me soup, medicine, and a healing blessing. The blessing told me things that I needed to know. The peace and comfort I felt was indescribable. Brother England was not only a philosopher, scholar, intellectual, and poet; he was a man of God—a spiritual beacon to us all.

John 8:32 says, "And ye shall know the truth and the truth shall make you free." Brother England helped me by teaching me to understand the definition of truth. Truth is not just "the facts," but it is our own experience and our own perspective of the facts. Gene taught me that through literature we can understand human nature, its complexities, its contradictions, its pains, and its joys. We don't live in a black-and-white, all-or-nothing world, and it is through literature that we can find real truth. He taught us that the scriptures are the greatest literature. Through them we can understand the struggle to become like Christ in a stressful, hate-filled world.

Many people discuss the factual accuracy of the Book of Mormon. To me it doesn't matter whether or not there is historical proof of the facts because the value of the Book of Mormon is in its literature and teachings. It, like the Bible, is a profound portrayal of human nature—our strengths and weaknesses with counsel on how to become happy and free through Christ. Jesus Christ was a rebellious, forward-thinking, compassionate son of God who taught through love, by example and through parables. Brother England and my mother, Mary Bradford, taught in poetry, which like parables, speaks directly to the spirit. I see no better way to learn.

Brother Eugene England, my mentor, lives on in spirit. He also lives on through his family. Katherine, his oldest child, has his independent spirit and leadership qualities. Jody has his creativity as well as his love for others and caretaking gifts. Mark, in addition to his artistic soul, has his ability to listen and give counsel without judgment. Jennifer has his fun-loving social skills and a smile to light a room. Becky has his quiet, reflective, spiritual nature with a combination of the intellectual and the religious. And last but not least, Jane has his understanding, love of the theatre, and his exuberance for life.

As wonderful as Eugene is, he is not without Charlotte. Charlotte has Gene's unique understanding of God and of people as evidenced in their own works of art, poetry, and other writings. She shares his qualities of love, intellect, compassion, and creativity. Gene and Charlotte are one.

Because of the England family, my life has more meaning. I am now a language arts tutor interested in instilling in my students a love of learning. I am also a dancer and "wanna-be poet." I value most my husband, my children, and my religion; they are my first priorities.

* * *

*One night at BYU I had a dream that I was dancing out in a field. A big white spaceship landed in front of me. The doors opened and Jesus came out with some of my teachers at BYU. One teacher taught us that all churches except ours would be damned. One teacher announced that a respected friend of our family was an antichrist. The campus psychologist, who was treating me for bulimia, told me to have an ice cream and call him in the morning. All of these men told me I couldn't board the ship because I had eaten far too many Twinkies and Hostess Cupcakes.*

*Later I had another dream where I encountered the same spaceship. This time Eugene England came out with Jesus as my personal Judge in Israel. He said, "We know about the Twinkies and Ding Dongs, and we know about your questions, doubts, and fears. Well done thou good and faithful daughter, you may enter in." I climbed onto the white spaceship to heaven, weeping.*

*Eugene England is to me what Lowell Bennion was to my mother—a teacher, an advisor, a Christlike example, and a friend.*

(This reflection was previously published in *Student Review*, 10 April 1998).

# Burnished with Hope

**SCOTT LIVINGSTON**

Scott Livingston is married to Ginger, and they live in Prairie Bush, Washington. They are the parents of four children and the grandparents of four granddaughters. Scott is a full-time writer. More of his writing can be found at brightmorningstar.substack.com.

During the semester that I was taking Gene England's Mormon literature class at BYU, I was dealing with all of the typical challenges that every poor college student struggles with. My wife, Ginger, was pregnant with our second child, and I was working part time at the MTC and making a whopping $3.35 an hour. I remember walking to and from the MTC, many days wondering how in the world we were going to make it. We lived in a tiny one-bedroom basement apartment next to the Provo City power plant. We had no phone, no furniture, little food, and abundant naiveté. But we were happy.

I was still struggling to learn how to be a student, and it showed in the quality of my performance. Sometimes I would turn in assignments late or not at all. (I still have dreams about that to this day.) I loved Gene's class and wanted to do my best work for him. I needed to know that someone believed in me more than I believed in myself. But I kept falling short.

On one particular occasion, we had an assignment to write a personal essay. I wish I could remember the subject. As had become my pattern, I waited until the last minute to write it and then had issues with my typewriter and had to do a lot of hand corrections, which made the essay both late and ugly.

Early the next morning I hustled up to the JKHB and made my way to Gene's office. I think I listened at the door just to be sure he wasn't inside. I scribbled a note on the front cover (pre-sticky-note days) with a no-doubt lame excuse about my typewriter or something, slipped the assignment under the door, and turned to run.

That's when the door flew open and Gene came running out, calling my name. I froze. This was my worst nightmare. Someone I looked up to and wanted so much to be like was now beholding my full-blown ineptitude. I slowly made my way back to him, expecting a reprimand (and deserving it) and quite possibly to be told that the assignment wouldn't be accepted.

Instead, this Christlike man looked into my soul with those beautiful, deep-set eyes and said, "Thank you. I'm excited to read this. When I'm done, can I bring it by your house so we can talk about it?" His offer fluttered in the air above me, a dove of grace. I melted. Likely I stuttered in undeserved wonder and said that such an offer was more than I could hope for. He smiled and said he'd be happy to help and expressed his confidence in me.

I walked out of the building different. Re-lit. Humming. Burnished with hope. It was a moment I've never forgotten.

Sometime after this, we were stunned to receive an invitation to Gene and Charlotte's home for a dinner. We were nobodies! I'm sure I wondered if he had mistaken us for someone else. I knew enough about the Englands at that point to know the kind of people I believed would qualify for a dinner invitation, and we were not that kind of people. I wish I could remember who was there. We felt so out of place at first, but the Englands were so good at putting people at ease. As we went home that night, I felt the same way I had when I had left Gene's office. I felt seen. I could even imagine that I might actually become something close to what I had so long wanted to be—someone with stories to tell and a purpose to fulfill. These experiences (and many more) happened more than twenty-five years ago, but the impression left by Gene and Charlotte is still vivid and resonant.

I know and have known many exceptionally good people whom I would consider "Christlike" in many ways. But there are just a handful that I would classify as true "saints," and Gene and Charlotte are on that list.

# An Angel Round About Me

**PATRICK Q. MASON**

Patrick Mason is a professor of religious studies and history at Utah State University where he holds the Leonard J. Arrington Chair of Mormon History and Culture. He is the author or editor of several books, including most recently (with David Pulsipher) *Proclaim Peace: The Restoration's Answer to an Age of Conflict.*

I never met Eugene England.

To my knowledge we were in the same room only once—on the evening of June 14, 1998. I was a student in Brigham Young University's London Study Abroad program, and Gene was in London at the same time directing a theater study abroad program. It was one of those providential "chance" encounters—I wasn't part of Gene's program, and it was my last Sunday in London before going home. I wrote this in my journal that evening:

> This afternoon, the Hyde Park Stake (of which we're a part) had a stake sacrament meeting, where they passed the sacrament to some 1,400 people. Afterwards, Bro Eugene England, director of the BYU theater program here, mediated a forum where people talked about their feelings about the 1978 revelation on priesthood. I was wary at first but became curious as to what would be said. I was impressed in that Bro England merely tried to dispel the two major myths that popular Mormonism has created to explain the reasoning for the ban (which reasons have never been spelled out in formal revelation to the Church), i.e., the less-valiant-in-the-pre-existence myth, and the Cain-Ham descent/cursing theory, both of which are contradictory to the fundamental principles of the gospel (namely, free agency and the nature of God) and unscriptural... What was best were the testimonies and insights of the many Black members who attended, providing shining examples of faith and perseverance.

My journaling voice was always a bit stiff, and I was less than a year off my mission, very much spiritually striving and suspicious of anything that fell outside institutionally approved channels. My memory of the event eclipses what I captured on the page. It's telling that of all the weekly firesides we had while I was in London, some of which I contemporaneously describe in more rapturous detail, this was the only one—and one of few of the scores of firesides I've attended throughout my life—that I still remember vividly.

I don't recall exactly what Gene said that night. What has always stayed with me instead is that Gene convened the fireside, which even then I recognized as something of a courageous act, and that he created and gave the space for Black members to share their own experiences without filter, correction, or judgment. For this white Mormon boy from the white Mormon suburb of Sandy, Utah, who served a mission in predominantly white Seattle, this may have been the first (and still today, a rare) time in my life when Black voices were privileged in a church meeting. Some of these sisters and brothers shared hard things. They shed tears. Some displayed anger. I didn't fully know how to process that as a twenty-one-year-old. Thus, all I could say—because it's practically all I *knew* to say—was how much I admired their "faith and perseverance."

Even at the time, however, I recognized that something more was at stake. Picking up from my expression of admiration for the Black members who spoke that night, my journal entry continued:

> There are many similar issues in the Church which are hard to answer and inspire high emotions, and I think it valuable to discuss them rather than repress them or consider legitimate questions (which we all have—that's the nature of not having sure knowledge) as expressions of doubt or apostasy. I feel it essential to root out the falsehoods that are so often prevalent in popular cultural Mormonism, but which are either unfounded in doctrine or blatantly contradictory to it. Many people get upset when you discuss such issues, often trying to justify shaky stances with isolated verses or the argument of "that's just the way it is," but I think that is one of the best indications that there is indeed an issue that needs to be dealt with and some questions and feelings that need resolution.

People sometimes ask me when I became sensitive to difficult questions about church history, doctrine, and culture, and how I developed a way of wrestling productively with those questions. No small part of that answer includes a June 1998 evening in London, when I came under the spell of Gene England and the community he gathered.

* * *

I don't have a corresponding journal entry that records when I first read Gene's classic 1986 essay, "Why the Church is as True as the Gospel." Whenever it was, it hit me like a lightning bolt then, and has rewarded me every time I have revisited it. Along with many others, I consider the essay to be one of the most scriptural things ever written that isn't canonized in scripture. It is a cornerstone of the case I made in my 2015 book *Planted: Belief and Belonging in an Age of Doubt*; quite honestly, I'm not sure I could have written my book had Gene not written his essay first. I've never read a better *apologia* for organized religion and organized Latter-day Saintism in particular. In my book I tried to muster a faint echo of what Gene had taught:

> The standard of the church's divinity is not its perfection but its ability to serve as a schoolmaster for gods in embryo. The things that may be most frustrating and perplexing may be the very means by which God is teaching us what it's like to be him. The church is not something we merely tolerate while striving to live the true gospel or anticipating the coming kingdom of God ... I believe that religion is meant to comfort the afflicted and afflict the comfortable—and that Mormonism is exceptionally good at both. Full participation in the church invites, even compels, me to have not just grudging tolerance for my fellow humans but to develop deep empathy and genuine charity for them, all while shining a light on my own flaws and hoping that others will forgive my many trespasses against them.

I wasn't trying to say anything particularly new so much as simply channel Gene's inspired insight for a new generation of readers.

* * *

Five years after that blessed night in London, I began a master's degree program in international peace studies at the University of Notre Dame. My interest in violent conflict and peacebuilding stems back to a transformational class I took with Professors Wilfred Griggs and Alan Keele as a freshman at BYU. But almost everything we read in that class was written by non-Latter-day Saints. And now as a graduate student I was devouring peace theology and other works on nonviolence from Christian scholars and luminaries such as Thomas Merton, John Howard Yoder, Walter Wink, Reinhold Niebuhr, Lisa Cahill, and, of course, Martin Luther King. Where in that grand chorus of Christian peacebuilders were the Latter-day Saint voices? I had come across a few of Hugh Nibley's somewhat scattershot writings on the topic, but the two Latter-day Saint texts that really gave me hope and courage were Elder Russell M. Nelson's October 2002 General Conference talk, "Blessed Are the Peacemakers," and Gene's underappreciated classic collection of essays called *Making Peace*.

Like Martin Luther King, Gene was not an absolute pacifist. But he did articulate an unflinching nonviolent ethic "which stands in judgment over all compromises we make with it." He reserved the right, for instance, to use force to repel a direct violent attack on his immediate family. In his mind, however, an ethic of nonviolence drawn from Latter-day Saint scriptures

> ... would call me to do everything possible, long before the attack, to avert the threat of attack (including building a less violent and sexist society where attacks on my wife and children would be less likely), to use an absolute minimum of violence, and to follow up with doing good to the victimizer as well as the intended victim ... The highest ethic would also serve as a constant reminder that I must try constantly not to dehumanize my enemy, to draw back as soon as possible, and to mourn rather than rejoice at my necessity.

When I wrote my first article about Latter-day Saint peacebuilding, "The Possibilities of Mormon Peacebuilding"—which I was proud to publish in *Dialogue*, the journal Gene founded—Gene's thinking featured prominently in my analysis. When Richard Bushman and I convened a conference on Latter-day Saint perspectives on war and peace, Gene's theology of peace was central in the conversation. When David Pulsipher and I would gather to discuss nonviolent Restoration theology while writing our book *Proclaim Peace*, we frequently invoked Gene's example, wisdom, and scriptural readings, even when we differed with some of his conclusions. David and I often quip that the Sermon on the Mount should be doubly important to Latter-day Saints because we have it twice in our scriptures. Gene wasn't perfect—no one, save the Prince of Peace, is. But I am convinced that for his sincere efforts to build peace in a world rife with conflict, Gene was and is truly one of "the children of God."

I never met Eugene England. But he has met me over and over again. He is, I believe, one of the angels God has sent to be "round about" me for the past quarter century. In whatever halting efforts I have made toward healing our racial divides, building the church as a sanctifying community of grace, and nurturing the seeds of a Restoration theology of peace, I've simply walked alongside my friend and mentor, Gene.

# July 22

## JAMES MCMICHAEL

James McMichael's most recent books of poems are *The World at Large*, *Capacity*, and *If You Can Tell*. He also wrote a book on James Joyce, *Ulysses and Justice*.

Gene England and I met sixty years ago as graduate students in English at Stanford. We began having almost daily talks. Six years older than I, he spoke with me always as a peer. Though I didn't know it at the time, I was learning with and (much more) from him how to come up with the best words. In the final essay of *Dialogues with Myself*, Gene confides to my eavesdropping a matter I wish he could hear back from me about. The melancholy of that wish I'll indulge here a little, even as I'll mostly be listening to him.

The essay is called "Enduring." He begins by saying he grew up in a safe valley, the composition of which he then evokes in detail for seven caressing paragraphs. We're told the history of its wheatfields' hydraulics and cultivation. Deer and trout were part of the fall diet along with farmed pig. Horses strayed and were gathered back. Each year there was the high-summer outdoor picnic and classes on that Sabbath which may have fallen at least once (though he leaves this to us to remember) on Gene's July 22nd birthday. Even within that safe valley he wanted "safe and secret places." These he searched out and discovered so his "mind would flow to a safe world inside" him. The ones he was most drawn to were those he made out of physical materials at hand: the canal he'd submerge in "with a straw for air," "pepper weeds three feet high," "the huge lilac clump at Dee's grandmother's" where he could be "completely hidden and watch crazy old Brother Nelson do his chores." It was there that he hid a revolver a friend had stolen from home and given him to keep. "One day it was gone."

After he situates his safe world in the broader terms of its geology on the map of southeastern Idaho, he tells us, "My father knew of larger things than our valley, and he included me easily." "I saw him doing the truth and felt safe." "One June dawn … he stopped the truck and took me to see how the wheat was heading out in that lower 320. We kept our feet between the rows as we walked out on a ridge, I just learning how to imitate his motion of plucking a stalk to examine critically its forming kernels. He asked me to kneel with him, and he spoke, I thought to Christ, about the wheat. He pledged again, as I had heard him at home, to give all the crop, all beyond our bare needs, to build the kingdom, and he claimed protection from drought and hail and wind."

Next to him there on the rows in the wake of his father's prayer, Gene felt beside and in him "something, a person, it seemed," something "warm like the sun," but warm inside his "head and chest and bones, someone like us but strange, thrilling, fearful but safe." "How is it then," he asks, "that sometime in those years" he felt for the first time his "own deepest, most hopeless, fear, the fear of being itself?" "It made no sense at all that anything should exist." From that time on, he writes, nothingness had "the better claim" than being. Its claim would "intrude" into his thinking whenever he left it. He "cannot imagine how . . . there could be something rather than nothing."

I'm not remembering how explicit Gene and I had been on being and nothingness back then, but it was a matter that grounded much of what we said to one another and asked. If he'd described persons as having a "constant yearning for meaning and permanence" as he does here, I'd have agreed with him. He and I *had* been explicit then about our being mortals for whom death would come like a thief in the night. And that the time was short. The valley I grew up in hadn't been safe. For me, being is what there is when beings that had come to light are no longer there. While love casts out fear, nothing on this side of my death am I able to acknowledge as permanent in relation to the oblivion that will be mine once I'm dead. Scripture tells me otherwise, and to know what I'm talking about here is of course impossible. I can't know what I'm talking about. I know I love my life to death. The apostle Paul helps me know there's nothing I have that I didn't receive. And I, who have much trouble believing, believe there will be no end soon to how long I'll go on being someone who'd lived and then died.

By nothing it's in
Death one's kept. One's kept
safe from Death by nothing.
They could be the parents.
To both of them one's owed.

For being kept safe
from and in Death by nothing,

thanks is waived
if God's called nothing.
Thanks be to

God one says
when nothing is instead called God
and of the farce that's Thanks for nothing
there's no strain.

Gene writes in "Enduring" that "the restored gospel provides the best answers . . . to the basic questions about how I came to be" as one of the mortal beings in being. The recent biographies of him couldn't be clearer about how much there was in the larger world that Gene's "moral courage" obliged him to collide with, nearly all of it compelling him "to examine critically its forming kernels" and be heard back from on what he understood it to be and to need. After I'd said goodbye to him in 1965, there wasn't a hint from him in our too-few meetings of what he'd done "to build the kingdom," of what his interactions with the leaders of his church had been, of all he was suffering and had suffered. A better friend to him than I was would have learned at least some of the headlines. I failed to.

He was a better friend to me. That was just like Gene. It had been fifteen years since we'd last met. That summer he managed to locate and stop by our phoneless cabin near Henry's Lake. My wife told him that if he drove twenty miles in the direction of the safe valley he'd soon write about, he'd find our car parked at the Harriman Ranch mailboxes one mile south of Last Chance. If the wind had come up by that time, I should be back to the road from the river in half an hour. I've lost how long it was Gene told me he and Charlotte had had to wait.

# I Am Still Inspired by His Words

**LUCY MORETON**

Lucy Wilkins Moreton is a 1961 graduate of the University of Utah in English education. She studied for her doctorate in theatre and philosophy until her chair died. She is a mother of five children and grandmother of twelve. These days she makes an earnest attempt to play both the silver flute and the Indian flute.

I first knew Gene England because my sister, Ann Wilkins Ellis, and her husband, Dick, were Charlotte and Gene's contemporaries in high school. They revered him then and later because of who he was and because of *Dialogue*'s impact on their lives. In 1963–65, Gene was my teacher in the Stanford Ward when my husband, Fred, was in school there. Later, my niece, Kathy Ellis Peterson, was in the group Gene led on a London study abroad trip in 1985. Kathy said that one day he shared some Lindor chocolates with everyone, saying, "All other chocolate will never be the same for you." She was a Hershey's gal but came to realize that he was teaching her not just about chocolate, but tasting, smelling, feeling, and knowing more deeply.

Gene was a man completely without guile, that rare being whose love and joy of life, Charlotte, and Jesus Christ were contagious. As a teacher and friend, he made me want to find and be the best person I could be. He encouraged me to draw from a deeper place inside—to be authentic in ways I had never explored before. Most of all, he encouraged me to stretch my humanity. He inspired me by his example to put Christ's gospel into practice. He did not just talk and write beautifully and profoundly, he acted on his words. An example is the planeload of humanitarian supplies he organized to send relief to Poland.

Gene had included Charlotte's nephew, David Oakey, on this trip because he spoke Polish and Gene intended to travel through the Iron Curtain into Poland. The group was stopped at the border and almost denied entry because of some church materials in their possession. It was mostly from their visit to Poland that I heard stories from Kathy about faith and freedom through Gene's generosity, curiosity, courage, and insight.

When my husband, Fred, and I floated down the Green River with Gene and Charlotte, I saw firsthand Gene as the consummate fisherman. I smile as I write this because his skills as fisherman took their inspiration not only from rivers but also from the Bible.

I can still see Gene's open face and boyish smile. I didn't always understand his keen, brilliant mind, but he was always accessible to my faltering attempts to understand.

Kathy said Gene was like a master gardener of perennials—planting seeds of ideas and thoughts that keep on growing with time and experience. One keeps returning to them as they grow deeper in color and blossom with the fragrance of meaning. I often felt tongue-tied and inadequate around him when his mind was galloping forward lickety-split, and my mind was trying to just stay in sight of where he started. But he instinctively seemed to have faith in me that maybe just the planting of those seeds might take root somewhere and blossom in my eternities. He made space for believers to question and space to know Christ, helping them to think beyond hard lines-in-the sand rules to a more compassionate Christlike place.

The principles and ethics Gene advocated for were troublesome to some, which caused him to suffer. I and others were bewildered that he was punished for wanting us to be more Christlike. He was the great example of enduring the criticism and rejection, teaching us how to respond with humility, kindness, and long-suffering. I am continuously grateful for his life, love, and influence and am still inspired by his words, even though … I am still running way behind.

# Eugene England and the Future of Mormonism

**BOYD PETERSEN**

*Boyd Petersen is the author of the award-winning biography* Hugh Nibley: A Consecrated Life *and the essay collection* Dead Wood and Rushing Water. *He has served as program coordinator of Mormon Studies at Utah Valley University, editor of* Dialogue: A Journal of Mormon Thought, *president of the Association for Mormon Letters, and book review editor of the* Journal of Mormon History.

My nearly-married and newly-married twenties were some of the most profoundly significant days of my life. Two events and two very different people were most influential to my way of living and thinking about Mormonism. The first event occurred on one of our first dates in 1983, when my then-fiancée, Zina, took me to a fireside sponsored by the BYU Honors Program. The speaker that night was English Professor Eugene England. Zina had taken an honors colloquium from Gene and raved about what an awe-inspiring teacher he was. But my initial impression of Gene was shock rather than awe. He began his lecture that night by talking about the Mountain Meadow's Massacre, the Willie and Martin Handcart Company, and the biblical narrative of Abraham's sacrifice of Isaac. Gene did not flinch from the troubling details. He told of the Mormons, following obediently their ecclesiastical leaders, and brutally killing the men, women, and children of the Fancher party. He discussed Levi Savage's passionate plea that the Willie Company wait until spring to cross the plains and how he was scolded by church leaders for not having enough faith. He discussed the two events in Mormon history as Abrahamic tests of integrity and faith. I remember growing increasingly uncomfortable as Gene continued, wondering to myself exactly what kind of fireside I was attending.

Then Gene switched gears, not abruptly, and not without fully forcing us to confront the horror of these stories. But he began to help us work toward a solution, a place where we could appreciate the paradoxical demands of personal integrity and obedience. I remember Gene reciting Joseph Smith's aphorism that "by proving contraries truth is made manifest" and assuring us that Mormonism requires us to unify heart and mind in order to find truth.

That fireside was a turning point in my life. Gene helped me to understand that faith and intellect are not two different realms—two separate spheres of the brain that must be shielded from each other—but that integration of the two is the only way for them both to be fully expanded. Intelligence broadens faith and faith broadens intelligence.

The other event occurred in April 1985. Zina—by then my wife of almost a year—and I traveled to Salt Lake City, hoping to attend General Conference. Unfortunately, we didn't get seats in the Tabernacle, but ended up listening instead as the conference was broadcast live in the Assembly Hall. One of the first speakers that Saturday morning was Elder Bruce R. McConkie who spoke of "The Purifying Power of Gethsemane." The soaring rhetoric of Elder McConkie's words coupled with his characteristic authoritative delivery left us all deeply moved by the sermon. As he concluded, Elder McConkie bore witness of Christ's divinity and Atonement and then, choking back tears, stated that "in a coming day I shall feel the nail marks in his hands and in his feet and shall wet his feet with my tears. But I shall not know any better then than I know now that he is God's Almighty Son, that he is our Savior and Redeemer, and that salvation comes in and through his atoning blood and in no other way." The atmosphere in the Assembly Hall was electric. I think all of us knew this would be Elder McConkie's last discourse and the poignancy of his confession of faith and the power of his witness moved us all. Less than two weeks later, Elder McConkie died. Elder McConkie's impact on me and my generation of church members cannot be overstated. He gave us a sense of surety that this church is divine, and he gave us doctrinal meat—speaking forthrightly, for example, about having one's "calling and election made sure"—rather than shallow platitudes. He inspired us to study the scriptures and to grow in the faith.

At the time Elder McConkie gave his last speech, Zina and I were both attending BYU and were members of the BYU 139th Ward. Our bishop was Eugene England. When we were searching for an apartment prior to our marriage, Zina wanted to find out the boundaries of the BYU 139th Ward, the ward where Professor England was bishop. All the cool people in the BYU Honors Program were moving into England's ward—some were attending who weren't even within the boundaries. Gene was a celebrity among what would now be called the "hipster" crowd. But I told Zina that I didn't believe in shopping for wards and felt that the Lord would place us where he wanted us. I don't know whether I was really persuasive or just exercised some unrighteous dominion, but we didn't shop for a ward. We moved into a small apartment owned by my aunt near the old pioneer-built Manavu Chapel just south of campus. When we met the other residents of the apartment, we discovered that we were in the 139th Ward. Zina won after all!

Gene was a bishop unlike any other I've had before or since. He was personally involved with each member of the ward. He got to know each of us by having all new couples attend the family relations class, which he taught. Gene used personal examples from his own marriage with Charlotte to illustrate each lesson, but his relationship with Charlotte spoke more than his words. They both seemed equally yoked and beautifully in love with each other.

Numerous times Gene counseled, comforted, and consoled Zina and me as we confronted the first painful moments of marriage when the blinding bliss fades and we started hurting each other. The ward had its challenges too. One young family was composed of two mentally disabled parents with one very brilliant five-year-old daughter. Gene called me to teach the Sunbeams, so I got to know the daughter quite well and saw firsthand how Gene worked to help this little family approach the problems of parenthood. I saw Gene's willingness to innovate in ways that personally involved each of us in the ward and inspired us all with his devotion to the gospel. We had Pioneer Day sacrament meetings outdoors in Provo Canyon. We had post-temple-night socials at the Englands' home with Charlotte's homemade ice cream. And best of all, we had weekly short sermons from Bishop England. It was a unique and wonderful experience, and I came to love Gene as a unique and wonderful man.

At the same time, I was enrolled in a Book of Mormon course taught by Elder McConkie's son, Joseph. There I found that same McConkie testimony and authority that inspired deeper scripture study and personal commitment. Both Bruce R. McConkie and Eugene England strengthened my testimony and shaped my life; however, the two were quite different in their approach to Mormonism. Indeed, several years prior to my experiences with them, Elder McConkie and Professor England had clashed in a series of private letters (one of which was leaked to the public and circulated widely). Claudia Bushman called the conflict between "the provocative thinker" England and "lawyer and doctrinaire General Authority" McConkie "a microcosm" of two strains within Mormonism: "between theological conservatives and liberals … and, in a larger sense, the tension between authoritarian control versus free expression." Indeed, the two men represent two starkly different visions of Mormon thought. Where Elder McConkie emphasized one set of absolute truths, Professor England stressed paradox and complexity. Where Elder McConkie taught unyielding obedience to institutional authorities, Professor England underscored the importance of exercising independent thought and maintaining personal integrity. Where Elder McConkie declared scriptural and prophetic authority, Professor England was interested in theological and intellectual exploration.

While both men influenced the way I think about and experience the church, I believe that the Mormonism of the future demands an approach more like Eugene England's than that of Elder McConkie's. In the internet age, where the free flow of information makes the possibility of a single correlated and controlled message about the church's teachings and history less and less possible, Elder McConkie's authoritarian style just doesn't work. But England's approach to the gospel can forestall the current exodus of disillusioned Mormons and, I believe, bring new converts into the church.

First, I believe Gene's vision of owning and confronting our past is critical. He understood that burying shameful history can lead not only to individual disillusionment and loss of faith, but also to institutional dishonesty. But Gene's honesty about our historical and theological history was not disinterested, nor disheartening. He loved examining the difficult choices members of the church confront because he saw that we each confront many of the same problems. If Levi Savage and the Mormons of Mountain Meadows had to confront the competing demands of obedience to authority and individual conviction on a grand scale, we each must do the same in our own lives. Gene didn't see white hats opposing black hats within the warp and weft of LDS history, but rather individual disciples forced to confront the demands of competing principles. He recognized that when obedience to authority wins, it sometimes comes at the expense of the individual heart; but when individual integrity wins, it can often come at the expense of community.

I believe Gene's emphasis on the individual paradoxes of human life, on the complicated real world of choices that each of us confronts, reflects the true nature of the world we live in. Certainly, there are moral "rights" and "wrongs" that church leaders have emphasized for so long, but more often we are confronted with more difficult choices. As Gene once wrote, "If we ... suppose there are easy solutions to the dilemma of personal integrity and social responsibility, we ... ultimately endanger our own salvation."

Gene's willingness to confront the hard truths of church history and theology did not leave him with a nihilistic view of the church. Instead, he celebrated the richness of Mormonism, and he loved the expansiveness of Mormon theology, of an eternity of learning and growing. He loved the compassion of a theology that postulates a God who weeps for his children and their trials. He also loved the epoch Mormon story of pioneer bravery and perseverance and implemented those pioneer ideals in his practical service to Food for Poland and in his nurturing care for his students and the ward he ministered to as bishop. Gene was full of optimism and delighted in spreading the gospel of peace.

Spreading that gospel, however, necessarily involves embracing diversity, and Gene believed that our very salvation depends on loving and accepting all God's children. "We can only know God as part of a triangular relationship that includes all other humans, his other children whom he loves as much as he does us," England argued. Differences between us—whether based on politics, religion, gender, race, or sexuality—should not divide us. Rather, Gene saw them as an essential resource for learning to be more like God.

Finally, Gene's vision of Mormonism was necessarily dialogic rather than dogmatic. This emphasis is, perhaps, the greatest difference between the world views of Professor England and Elder McConkie. They were both true believers, they both loved the gospel, and they both saw themselves as consecrating their gifts of heart and mind to the church. But where England embraced difference and nurtured discussion, McConkie sought conformity or silence. As England's daughter, Rebecca, has written, "One approach invites dialogue; the other silences dissent." In the age of the internet, a dialogic approach to the gospel is the only possible approach.

Eugene England's vision of the gospel was expansive enough for the age of the internet because he understood that Mormon discipleship requires the devotion of both heart and mind. Orson Scott Card once wrote about the "prophetic" quality of Eugene England's writing, "If you place yourself in his hands and receive his words with an open, undefended heart, he will bring you closer to the Spirit of God and closer to the community of Saints."

The words of both Elder McConkie and Eugene England brought me closer to the Spirit of God and closer to the community of Saints, but the future of Mormonism, I believe, requires us to embrace an approach to the gospel closer to that of England's.

# Remembering Gene

**LEVI S. PETERSON**

Levi Peterson currently lives in Issaquah, Washington, with his wife, Althea. He taught English at Weber State University in Ogden, Utah, for thirty-five years and was granted emeritus status upon his retirement.

There was a calm, almost prosaic quality about Gene—an unassuming, everyday kind of demeanor that could easily lead one to ignore the reality that there was also a true saintliness about him. Saintliness is a dubious quality to attribute to anyone. It implies a terrifying rigor, an uncompromising surrender of the self to God's ways and wishes. One way to achieve saintliness is to define it downward. Being a Mormon of record, even a slouching, dilatory keeper of the commandments like myself qualifies. I am afraid that all too often even those who believe themselves qualified candidates for the title of saintliness have missed its point. But Gene, yes, I'll vote for his saintliness.

I first became intimately acquainted with Gene and Charlotte when, early in 1991, they joined a writing group to which Althea and I belonged. On a Sunday evening in March of 1992, we drove to Provo to attend a session of this writing group at the home of Gene and Charlotte. It was our custom that the writer at whose home we were assembling distributed a manuscript in advance, which, following dinner, we critiqued. On this occasion, the manuscript was an essay Gene had written entitled "Monte Cristo," which was about a day's fishing trip he and Doug Thayer made to the South Fork of the Ogden River, which drains a watershed capped by a peak named Monte Cristo, a term translating into English as something like "Christ's Mount."

Before Gene's advent into our group, it had been the custom for the featured writer to listen quietly for at least a half hour, hopefully learning thereby how his or her piece struck its readers. Gene, however, had little patience with this custom. On this particular evening, he intervened in our discussion soon after it had begun, asserting that we were failing to grasp its Christian import. I remonstrated, saying that the text offered no more than a pleasant narrative about a fishing excursion of two friends. I said that if Gene wished his reader to interpret the narrative as an allegory for a Christlike relation between human beings, he needed to say so expressly, a suggestion

Gene dismissed with an annoyed wave of his hand. This annoyed me in turn because it seemed to imply that a reader of this essay who needed an explicit statement was something less than competent.

Later in the evening, returned to Ogden, I vented my spleen in my diary by derisively calling Gene "the Great Christian." Then, even as I prepared to write the next sentence, I repented of my petulance and admitted that, despite his inability to listen to how others were interpreting his sentences, Gene was indeed the Great Christian, certainly the greatest I have known personally. I expressed the essence of Gene's saintliness in my diary with these sentences: "Gene lives, eats, breathes the commandment to love one another. He suffers over conflict of all kinds, from war to backbiting."

Gene was an activist in good causes. I confess that I was only half aware of these over the years because he never talked about them in my presence. It was the outpouring of appreciation for Gene in the months following his death that instructed me how widely he engaged in and recruited others to engage in a variety of charitable campaigns and protests against war and weaponry.

The quality of Gene's saintliness that I knew most intimately was his profound, instinctive, unyielding belief in the good to be found in human beings. It was a quality I felt simply by being in his presence because I could discern that he was applying it to me. The Christ of the Apocalypse, astride a white horse and attired in a vesture dipped in blood, the Christ who judges and makes war, was not Gene's Christ. Gene's Christ told an adulteress to go her way and sin no more.

I have referred to myself as a backslider over and over in the purlieus of liberal Mormonism. It was, however, a term Gene refused to concede to me. He wouldn't accept that I was a sham Christian. The mere fact that he spoke with me so often, so easily and congenially, with such open acceptance, testified as to the worth he discerned in me. The most important thing about Gene for me was that he made me feel more like a true Mormon. In his presence, I felt my inadequacies diminished and my qualities enhanced. God be thanked for the life and influence of Gene England.

# Reaching Out, Building Relationships

**CHARLES AND KATHLEEN PETTY**

Chuck and Kathy (aka Charles and Kathleen) live in Bellevue, Washington, where Charles is a retired physician and Kathleen is an active gardener.

During the first week of my first year at Stanford, I got a call saying that there was someone waiting in the lobby to talk to me. That someone was Gene England, who had come to invite me to a freshman seminar he was leading that year called "Literature and Christianity." It was to be held once a week in his home, and he was making an effort to personally invite all the incoming freshmen. At the time I didn't think too much about such an invitation from an Institute teacher identifying the incoming Mormon freshmen to a weekly gathering in his home, hoping to excite them about a topic that was dear to him. I also didn't think about how Charlotte was dealing with the homework and bedtime routine of six children by herself while all this went on in her living room. There were six to ten of us who met, some more regularly than others. I can remember we read *The Brothers Karamazov* and *The Plague*, among other books. Not everyone in the group was interested in literature, but, looking back, I suspect the topic was secondary. Gene was interested in building relationships among the students and with the students. He wanted to make sure there was someone available to listen in the event of a religious crisis, or just to talk about "issues."

It was a turbulent time at Stanford. The university had decided not to include BYU on its basketball schedule because of the LDS church's teaching that Blacks could not hold the priesthood. The Vietnam War was heating up, and the church's stand on it was conservative. And it was the beginning of the sexual revolution. I was not the only person among my freshman peers who was coming from a placid high school experience to a campus roiling with new ideas and energy.

I remember subsequent Institute classes taught by Gene that took us through the scriptures that were used to back the church's stand on the priesthood-and-the-Blacks issue. He was honest about his feeling that the scriptures didn't support the ban, yet he was clear also about his testimony. It was evident that these issues were as important to him as they were to us. He sponsored a "Day of Concern" at the Institute, and he invited Neal Maxwell to come talk with us about these issues and how we could make a difference.

Gene also invited us students over for dinner. He always had a few stray students at his Thanksgiving table. He reached out in many ways. He was intense but he also laughed a lot. He had unlimited energy, which we seemed to take for granted.

About this time, my relationship with Gene and Charlotte became more personal because I married Chuck Petty, whose friendship with Gene predated my coming to Stanford. Since they were friends, Gene and Charlotte generously included me in that friendship. They even made the trip to Salt Lake for our wedding.

Chuck and I became sometime-babysitters. We were invited to hang around the *Dialogue* offices, offer an occasional student perspective on papers, or just stuff envelopes. We were invited to go to Bearmont—that England family refuge in the redwoods where there was always some kind of building going on that seemed totally disorganized to me. We witnessed the first signs of Charlotte's feminism. Sitting around their kitchen table, she mentioned with great difficulty how hard it was to see how much Gene spent on books when there were other things she wanted money for. I remember how intently Gene listened, not interrupting or offering comments. I remember excellent children's art on the refrigerator, and how I naively said if Charlotte didn't want that great picture of a dragon that Jennifer had drawn, I would love to have it.

The final crucible of our friendship with Gene and Charlotte, the event that melded us together, was the epic trip to Minnesota where Gene had accepted a position at St. Olaf's College in Northfield. They were trying to figure out how to move their possessions and their family when they had no money. Chuck offered to drive a U-Haul. We would caravan with them to Salt Lake, and then on to Minnesota. There was a revolving combination of kids with drivers; in the end it was Gene and Charlotte with their kids in the station wagon, and Chuck and I in the truck. I should probably mention the car-sick cat and the night all ten of us spent in one room in a motel somewhere between Salt Lake and Northfield.

We saw their first house in Northfield. I recall it was surrounded by trees and that Kathryn, their oldest, got the bedroom that seemed like a treehouse because the windows that went to the floor were practically inside a tree. A neighbor came right over with some sweet corn. Gene and Charlotte took us out to dinner to say thanks, and flew us back to Utah.

Over the year, in Utah and elsewhere, our lives have continued to cross, always with a renewal of the rich friendship we have enjoyed.

# A Life of Love

**GREGORY REECE**

Gregory Reece was born in Provo, Utah, raised in Orem, and then whisked to the suburbs of Minneapolis midway through high school. In college he abandoned the engineering track that his father had him on and dove into the performing arts—especially dance and theater. He chose to move to New York City over Los Angeles and initially found work in the cable business, then later moved into production of documentary films. When freelancing did not bring in a living wage, he somehow fell into banking, from which he retired five years ago. He now shuttles between his Brooklyn apartment and a house in the Catskill Mountains, enjoying the riches of both places.

The attribute of Gene's that stands out most to me is his love. At first, I was struck by the love that he shared with his wife, Charlotte, and the love that they showed to their children. Then I felt that love directed to me and others in the small Minnesota branch where I met him when I was a college freshman at Carleton College, near St. Olaf's College in Northfield, where Gene had recently taken a position. Gradually, I saw how his love extended to a wide network of friends and colleagues, spilling over to include acquaintances and even strangers that I saw him encounter in the New York subways and on London streets. I watched him and marveled at his patience and the interest that he took in others wherever he went, no matter where he was or who the person was.

That love was different from what I had experienced in my life, and, like many others, I was drawn to the England family. As I prepared to leave home for college I looked forward to the academic opportunities at Carleton, but wondered if church would be an option. As Sunday approached the first week at school, I checked the phonebook to see if there was a ward or branch nearby. Calling the listed number, I was offered a ride to church by the branch president and his wife, Brother and Sister Kenknight.

The branch met in a makeshift chapel in the upper room of Joe's Bar in downtown Fairbault, Minnesota. The location could not have been more incongruous. Cleaning up the space after Saturday night revels fell to the Kenknights and anyone else on hand to help them. That first week, we arrived early, and Sister Kenknight dashed around collecting armloads of empty beer bottles and dropping them, clattering, into waiting garbage cans. Meanwhile, President Kenknight emptied ashtrays and opened the windows to clear out the smell of cigarette smoke and stale beer. They handed me a broom, and I attempted to sweep up. When it came time to start the meeting, the room was a bit cleaner, but the temperature was so low that we had to keep our coats on during the service.

Disheartened by the cleanup, the service didn't do much to lift my spirits. The branch seemed to be hardly functioning. Between meetings, I stood at the front of the makeshift chapel looking out the window, feeling quite discouraged, when a man came up to me and said, "Hi, I'm Gene England." He told me that he had just started working at St. Olaf's College. A week or so later, Gene spoke in sacrament meeting, and it became apparent to me that he would be put in charge. Sure enough, three weeks later he was called to be branch president.

Gene immediately reorganized the branch presidency, including calling Sister Kenknight to be the branch clerk, largely because she knew everyone on the branch roster. Gene pointed out that she might have been the only female clerk in the church. Her given name was Frances, and no one mentioned that she was a woman when her name was submitted for approval.

Gene soon implemented a schedule for the congregation to read a set number of pages in the Book of Mormon each week, to be discussed by the branch presidency at the following week's service. Gene rotated the teaching with his counselors, but if either was absent, he was always ready to substitute.

Soon I heard that Gene, or others on his behalf, were making calls to Salt Lake to get approval to buy an empty building to convert into a meetinghouse. In passing, I overheard comments about how the church building bureaucracy was pushing for one kind of structure in town, while Gene had proposed another in a much more bucolic setting. To me it seemed inevitable that the church's plan would prevail, so I was amazed when the word came down that the church agreed to purchase an abandoned schoolhouse, outside of town, surrounded by woods and cornfields. I doubt that I was the only one in the branch to ask, "How did he do that?"

With the necessary approvals in place, Gene enlisted skilled branch members in designing and making the building function as a Latter-day Saint meetinghouse. Meanwhile, he and Charlotte scoured secondhand shops in the surrounding countryside and found a dozen or so carved oaken pews and a pulpit with carved *alphas* and *omegas* from decommissioned or closed churches.

In a matter of months, we were meeting in an attractive chapel with a slightly raised stand and soothing light yellow-green walls that reflected the springtime colors in the neighboring fields. The pews were put into service and the pulpit stood solidly at the front edge of the stand, with the *alphas* and *omegas* removed, though their outlines remained plainly visible, much to my amusement.

The branch covered a large multi-county area, and even though there were hundreds of members on the rolls, only thirty or forty attended meetings. Gene devised a plan whereby either he and his counselors or he and Charlotte would contact every member of the branch at least quarterly. In his indomitable Chevrolet, Gene and his various companions traveled the country back roads looking for members. Of course, on the way, Gene took in the local sights and returned with engaging stories and items of interest. Locals commented often that the Englands knew more about the surrounding area than most people who had lived there all their lives.

One could tell that Gene thought a lot about the branch. In fact, it would be easy to think that it was his full-time job. Conducting meetings, he would regularly relate something that he learned about various members of the branch, such as their interests, service, or accomplishments. This opened my eyes and sparked my interest in members with whom I otherwise would not have had much interaction. Those introductions helped us change from a disparate, seemingly unrelated group of people into a vibrant, loving congregation.

One day after having had Sunday dinner at their home, Gene and Charlotte dropped me off at my dormitory. As we sat in the car finishing our conversation, the topic of Blacks and the priesthood came up. I regurgitated the standard myth about Black people being less faithful in the preexistence. Gene listened and then calmly stated that the teaching had no basis in scripture or revelation. Shocked, I responded with anger at the teachers and leaders I felt had misled me. Gene quietly said that it was not their fault, that they were merely teaching something that they had been taught. At the time it struck me how calmly he stated the facts of the issue. He didn't try to convince me or recruit me to his side, nor did he speak ill of those who thought differently than he did. Over the years, as I learned how strongly he opposed the policy of keeping Black men from the priesthood, I became even more impressed with how simply he explained the facts to me and left me to draw my own conclusions.

Another attribute of Gene's that stands out for me was his undeterred faith in God. Gene's belief went beyond intellectual interests and pursuits, as evidenced by his deep faith and dedicated participation in the church. He understood such participation as God's way of helping us learn to work with, love, and care for each other. Gene took his church callings as seriously as any professional pursuit.

His passion seemed directly connected to his concept of God. Some people might disagree with him, but Gene believed that God not only wanted, but needed us, his children, for his own eternal life, suggesting the potential, and even possibly the necessity, of learning from each other.

That connection or shared need between God and individuals seemed not just an idea or principle for Gene, but a way of life. He seemed to live in a different dimension than most. He didn't see the need to control or contain people, especially in an organization as large as the church. Instead, he hoped to open their minds and eyes to see what was possible and encourage them to grow into it.

If he used any power or force to persuade people, it was the power of love. No doubt, he could argue with the best of them, but he knew that had only a limited effect. He also knew the limitations of dictums. He knew that through love mighty works were possible, and he worked to keep that the focus. He was a strong advocate for all of us to love one another, and he demonstrated it powerfully through his example.

Being a recipient of his love has had an enormous impact on my life, and for that I am grateful. This is not to say that Gene was perfect. He could exploit the connections he had with people at times, especially to enlist their help on incredible projects, like building a cabin or a remarkable home, or collecting food to help the people in Poland. Still, as much as Gene asked of anyone, he gave back in bucketloads.

Gene always had a way of making the most of anything he put his mind to, and it was always a great learning experience to go on adventures with him. I love and miss him very much and look forward to hearing all that he has learned, and seeing what he has found, in the next life.

# Talking and Listening to Gene

**ROBERT A. REES**

Robert "Bob" Rees is an independent scholar, poet, university professor, and humanitarian. He is the former director of Mormon Studies at Graduate Theological Union and the co-founder and vice president of the Bountiful Children's Foundation. He is the editor of *Proving Contraries: A Collection of Writings in Honor of Eugene England* (Signature, 2005).

"In the beginning was the dialogue."
(Hugh Nibley's translation of John 1:1)

"To me, dear friend, you never can be old."
—Shakespeare

Gene England loved nothing better than to have a good dialogue—to talk with and listen to others and to engage in interesting conversations, even with strangers. As with many who were fortunate enough to call him friend, he and I had hundreds of talks over the course of our friendship. His talk was never idle or lazy but always informed by his good mind and good heart, his insatiable curiosity, his universal interest in people and ideas, and his boundless enthusiasm. As perhaps the most influential Mormon intellectual of his generation, Gene was never bored or boring. As he said in the essay that introduced him to the wider Mormon community, "The Possibility of Dialogue: A Personal View," "My faith encourages my curiosity and awe; it thrusts me out into relationship with all the creation." The word "thrusts" says it all.

Our first talk took place sometime in 1967 or 1968, not long after I started teaching at UCLA. I had written to Gene expressing my interest in helping with *Dialogue*. He asked me (along with Karl Keller) to edit a special issue of the journal devoted to Mormon literature (1969). It was during this time that I went to Stanford to meet Gene for the first time. That first meeting was the beginning of countless conversations and a lifelong friendship.

When I think of Gene, I think of the cover of that inaugural issue of *Dialogue*: a drawing of two people conversing under a tree. That conversation symbolizes what I came to value most in Gene—a man eagerly engaged in dialogue—with himself, with others, and with God—in fact, with anyone who had honest questions or something interesting to talk about. What was gratifying for me is that I felt there was nothing that we couldn't talk about. He was a wonderful conversationalist not only because he loved exchanging ideas with others but also because he was such a good listener. I never felt with Gene, as I have with some and as I have observed in my own conversational style, a half-listening while preparing a response. And I never found him negative about any new idea. He loved nothing more than to participate in what the Anglo-Saxons called *umbesitendas*, a group of friends sitting around a fire or mead table sharing stories and telling tales into the night.

Recently, in listening to recordings of Gene and rereading his articles, essays, and poems, many of our conversations came flowing and sometimes flooding back to my memory. In rereading his essay "Enduring," I was reminded of a particular conversation we had. I don't remember exactly when or where it took place, but, as often happened, it was a free-ranging conversation involving lots of ideas and issues. Somehow, it turned to deeper matters and to a subject I had spoken about only once or twice in my life—that at times, usually in the middle of the night, I find myself caught between two equally frightening ideas—that at some point our existence will end with absolute finality—and, equally frightening, that it will never end! I recounted a conversation I had had many years previously with my youngest son, Maddox, when he was six or seven. He had come into my bedroom long after he should have been asleep and in a frightened voice said, "Dad. I've been thinking. We go to sleep and we wake up and we go to sleep and we wake up and we do it over and over and over; it goes on and on forever and it never ends!" I pulled him into bed and held him tightly and said, "I know what you mean. I have thoughts like that myself sometimes and they are really scary." After telling this story to Gene, he was quiet for a moment and then he said, "I didn't realize anyone but me had such thoughts. At times when I think about these things, I feel as if I am approaching the edge of madness, and I have to quickly do something to distract myself." Which is exactly what I do in such moments.

I had forgotten this conversation until reading the following passage in "Enduring" in which Gene recounts such recurring feelings dating from his childhood in Southern Idaho's Marsh Valley:

> How is it that sometimes in those years I first felt my own deepest, most hopeless fear, the fear of being itself? It is a fear I have never been able to write about until now nor imagined anyone else knew about or could understand, a fear so fundamental and overwhelming that I feel I must literally shake myself from it when it comes or go mad.

Such darkness of soul is captured in Robert Frost's "Desert Places," where the poet faces an inner and outer world of stark, absolute aloneness. He says,

They cannot scare me with their empty spaces
Between stars—on stars where no human race is.
I have it in me so much nearer home
To scare myself with my own desert places.

What rescued Gene (and me and others) from such desert places is the realization that he could make meaning and beauty even in a world that sometimes seems absurd and meaningless, that words to express such dark thoughts were themselves a counter testament, especially when they were used to explore and describe the world that lies beneath and beyond the blackness. Thus, in the same essay we find such dark-defying language as the following:

> I could sometimes stop and hide for a time under the sagebrush out of the wind. I could crush the small gray-green, velvet leaves from the strangely dead-looking branches until the air was sharp with sage or hold my fingers close until the smell went back into my throat . . . And by late May a few wild honeysuckles, the blossoms washing pink and detachable, made to be plucked off delicately and delicately set between the lips so the tube under the blossom could be sucked for the smallest, most delicate taste, deep on the tongue.

Remembering delight in the aroma of crushed sagebrush leaves and the sweet taste of honeysuckle blossoms while writing an essay about the deepest darkness of spirit says a lot about the kind of man and poet Gene England was—but it doesn't say all. He was also a Christian humanist, a man astraddle (and that's the right word) the rational and the spiritual, the secular and the sacred, the human and the divine. That's why, in the same essay, he also speaks of finding both dependence and identity in God, of having, in his words, "felt confirmed in my own separate, necessary, and unquenchable being," of finding in the restored gospel the "best answers—the most adventuresome and joyful—to the basic questions about how I came to be here and about my present and future possibilities."

That was one of Gene's many dialogues with himself. As Gene said in his introductory essay in *Dialogue*, he was guided by his commitment to Christ and his gospel and rooted in his Mormonness: "But my very grasp on this specific direction, this 'iron rod,' turns me out to all people and their experience in desire for dialogue with them." That turning out (and toward) all people, that desire for dialogue with them, was what attracted so many people to Gene. He was always willing to talk, and to listen, to *engage*, and the range of his intellect, compassion, curiosity, and commitment was large. That largeness has left a giant absence in my heart, but also a sweet longing for that endless time in the eternities when we will resume our conversation that was interrupted by his untimely death.

I miss Gene immensely. I have a frequent longing to talk to him. I want to know what he thinks and feels about so many things, including so many that have happened since his passing—9/11, the war in the Middle East, Obama, Trump, COVID-19, and, as I write this, the Russian invasion of Ukraine. I also have a longing to talk with him about what is happening within our religious community, especially the challenges faced by so many young Latter-day Saints, the kinds of challenges he had in mind when he began *Dialogue*.

I look forward to the time when, as Melville wrote to his close friend Hawthorne, "We shall sit down in Paradise, in some little shady corner by ourselves, [where] we shall cross our celestial legs in the celestial grass … and pleasantly discourse on all the things manifold which now so distress [and excite] us." That would be lovely beyond any singing of it.

# Increasingly Kindred Souls

**THOMAS ROGERS**

Thomas Rogers was emeritus professor of Russian language and literature at BYU as well as an LDS missionary and patriarch, essayist, and playwright.

I believe that Eugene England and I were (are) increasingly kindred souls. Gene spoke truth to power and paid a price for it, while I merely wrote plays about other actual people who, like Gene, did the same. In his introduction to the third volume of my nineteen published plays collection, *The Plays of Thomas F. Rogers: Crises in Faith* (Newport, Me: Leicester Bay Theatricals), my former BYU student actor and colleague playwright, Scott Bronson, recalls that on one occasion during a gathering at the Church Office Building of "Mormon artists of various and varied stripes," which I barely recall, I apparently commented that "all art is subversive." "Even the figures lurking at the edge of the room moved in," Scott writes. "'What do you mean by that?' Tom was asked. 'Only that all art is designed—or should be designed—to challenge our views of life and the world around us. It should always have as its primary goal the challenging of our hearts and minds.'" Gene England's art of expression in his essays and his activism did just that.

I may have met Gene long before most of those who first knew or knew of him after he founded *Dialogue* while a graduate student at Stanford. After his family had moved to Salt Lake City from Idaho, we both joined the debate club at East High School, and later at The University of Utah's LDS Institute of Religion, I sat near Gene and Charlotte in the classes of their, my, and my future wife Merriam's especially influential mentor, Lowell Bennion. After my first mission (to Germany), Gene and Charlotte had returned from their joint mission to Samoa to The University of Utah, where, in his senior year, Gene edited the student literary journal, *The Pen*, in which he published the account of my unprecedented ten-day train trip from Berlin to Moscow while still serving as a missionary assigned to Germany. (Although this was with my mission president's kind permission, Gene discretely omitted any reference to my having done so as a missionary.)

Years after Gene joined the English faculty at BYU, our paths often crossed. However, regretfully, although I was aware of his polemical activity, he and I never engaged in any deep conversations. We were rather like "ships passing in the night," each pursuing his particular discipline and interacting with his own students and fellow teachers. Nor was I a fisherman like Gene, his colleague, Douglas Thayer, and their department chair, Bert Wilson, Gene's boyhood friend. I now envy their forays to the nearby canyon streams and the talk they engaged in there. With the soirees they regularly held in their Provo home for any and all in the campus community, Gene and Charlotte were exceptionally sociable and inviting. They even featured a reading of my stage adaptation of Dostoevsky's *Crime and Punishment* just before it played in the Harris Fine Arts Center.

Because of my knowledge of Polish and my earlier residences in Warsaw and Gdansk, Gene asked me and a few others to join him in promoting his remarkable Food for Poland endeavor after the Solidarity movement's shipyard riots during that country's communist domination. I actually did very little to assist but marveled at Gene's effectiveness in arranging the shipment of containers of foodstuffs for the unionists and their families. Unexpectedly, Charlotte, Gene, and another faculty couple, Garold and Norma Davis, also helped defray our expenses as Merriam and I prepared for our mission call to the Russia St. Petersburg Mission. Gene had assigned the reading of my plays in his BYU courses on Mormon literature and—deserved or not—wrote the accolade at the 1998 Mormon Festival Arts award ceremony in St. George in which he cites me as "undoubtedly the father of modern Mormon drama," which remains an especially endearing compliment.

Like Lowell Bennion, that is how Gene was toward so many others—his students, readers of *Dialogue*, those he served as a bishop, and many more. Knowledgeably crossing swords regarding the origin and values of our faith with some of the church's principal spokespersons during those doctrinally dogmatic years, Gene remains a Latter-day Saint legend, the devout "father of progressive Mormonism."

# For Gene—Because He Has Given Much

**KAREN ROSENBAUM**

After a rewarding thirty-four years conducting classes in a California community college, Karen Rosenbaum retired to do what she loved even more than teaching: not teaching. She has been able to spend time on assorted writing and editing projects, including a collection of short fiction, *Mothers, Daughters, Sisters, Wives*. She is a member of the extraordinary Berkeley First Ward.

It was during the 1961–62 school year, in the publications wing of the old University of Utah Union building, that I first met Gene England. I was what my husband refers to as a "white shoe," one of those students frenetically involved with campus activities (some of which required uniforms, and at least one of which required white oxfords). As a member of the publications council, I got to know Gene in his capacity as student activities advisor. A gentle, patient man, he would build us up and calm us down. I would graduate that June in English; Gene had earned his U of U English degree four years earlier. I was delighted to discover that we both had applied to Stanford for graduate work. Gene would, appropriately enough, pursue a doctorate in English with a Danforth Fellowship, which assumed—rightly—that he was "aware of the place for moral and religious values in teaching and counseling." My fellowship had no moral and religious strings attached. I was aiming for a master's degree with a creative writing emphasis; I would be working with two former Utahns, Richard Scowcroft and Wallace Stegner.

Stanford students—undergraduate, graduate, single, married—all attended the same ward in those years. I would see Gene and Charlotte and the kids—four of them at that time—in church. I would also see them in their home, where I was invited for dinners and allowed to babysit. And I would see Gene in the English graduate study on the Stanford Quad. Before, between, and after my classes, I would plop down at the front table, opposite Gene, and spread my books out—a much smaller array than those spread out in front of him. I would complain about my required Anglo-Saxon class and the poetry class in which Yvor Winters dogmatically ranked all the poets and excoriated all the students. I would relate my anxiety about the creative writing seminar, where I was the youngest and least experienced of the twelve participants and where the only other woman was already a much-published writer who read us clever stories about editing textbooks and writing greeting cards. I adored Wallace Stegner, a father figure for me my first extended time away from home. Gene would be my big brother figure. There, in the graduate study room, I would share with him my academic and romantic and religious ordeals. He never told me he was too busy to listen. Incidentally, I personally only knew one student whom Yvor Winters liked: Gene. The rest of us, Winters never tired of telling us, were vastly inferior to the goats he kept in his backyard.

Gathered on folding chairs in a small room in the old Student Union building one afternoon, a dozen of us listened as Gene played for us a tape he cherished. Speaking was Paul Tillich, the Protestant theologian and philosopher, who taught at the University of Chicago. I can't pretend to have understood most of Tillich's remarks, which seemed to me abstract and were delivered in a heavy German accent, but I will always remember Gene's passion for Tillich, who died during Gene's years at Stanford. Gene could be defined by his passion for good things that he could share.

I left Palo Alto the summer of 1963, having promised Mr. Stegner that I would send him the short stories for my thesis, a promise I kept. In the crevices of my memory are boxes, many boxes, I sent back to Utah with the Englands, in exchange, I think, for the bicycle I had ridden to campus every day. Later I found out that the Englands had to rent a U-Haul to transport my things—and that Jody, riding the bicycle to her piano lesson, ran into a parked car. She wasn't seriously hurt, but the bicycle-box deal was not a favorable transaction for the Englands.

When I returned to Palo Alto after a three-year hiatus, *Dialogue* was taking root in Wes Johnson's campus office. Worried that I might starve on the meager pay of my temp jobs, Gene created for me the position of "office manager," which I executed in such a way that no one but me could find anything. The Englands had six kids by then, and they hired me to take care of four of them—Jody, Mark, Becky, and baby Jane—for a week while they took Kathryn and Jenny to Utah. I don't know that the children exactly thrived that week, but we all survived.

After I moved to the East Bay in 1966, I would frequently return to the peninsula to visit my friends. Gene was a bishopric counselor, and I'm sure he counseled the bishop, but he also spent a great deal of time counseling students. He also spoke at *our* Institute, the home of the Berkeley student ward, attracting many young people who were trying to make sense of their lives. Members of the Berkeley University Ward at that time included Scott Kenney and Peggy Fletcher, who were working on a new fringe publication, *Sunstone*, and Bonnie Bobet, who organized one of the first Sunstone-like symposia in the Bay Area. At the end of one of Gene's Berkeley presentations, he pulled out his checkbook, wrote a check (it seemed to me a *large* check) to show his support for the new magazine, and encouraged us to do the same.

One of the things I most looked forward to at the Salt Lake Sunstone symposia over the years was seeing Gene and Charlotte. When Gene told me that, since I lived in a Democratic enclave, I should register as a Republican, I retorted that he, once again a Utahn, should therefore register as a Democrat. The Englands were good friends with Marlene and Wayne Owens, Utah's Democratic Congressman for eight years, and I teased Gene about his party affiliation when the Owenses sat with the Englands at the Saturday evening Sunstone dinner. Besides, Gene's views on so many issues aligned with those in the Democratic Party.

Those views often did not align with those of the church hierarchy and education systems. I was one of the outraged when I learned of the injustices Gene suffered, especially at BYU. Some were even critical of the Food for Poland campaign the Englands organized in the 1980s, when political repression meant that countless Polish citizens were hungry. How, I thought, could anyone question the purity of Gene's ardor to relieve suffering?

In 1993, accompanied by my husband, I led my California college's small study abroad troop to Stratford-upon-Avon for a semester. By then, Gene and Charlotte were old hands at traipsing about London with college students—and often their own children. I could barely keep track of the fourteen students under my care; Gene had two to four times that many in a city close to three hundred times more populous and dangerous than Stratford. (My students, however, had not signed on to the BYU honor code.)

The hymn "Because I Have Been Given Much" could be Gene's theme song. He could not see another's lack and not share his and Charlotte's glowing fire, loaf of bread, roof's safe shelter overhead.

Yes, 2020 and 2021 were very difficult years. But for me the year 2001 was memorable in the most painful ways. There was the awfulness of 9/11. Later that month, my dear friend, Bonnie Bobet, succumbed to acute myelogenous leukemia. And the month before, on August 20, I wrote in my journal, "Gene died Friday—August 17. I didn't tell Bonnie. She needn't know that now."

I am older than Gene got to be. How much he helped so many! How many more he would have helped had he been allowed to live longer. I am flawed in character and feeble in faith. But I know that Gene would even now regard me as a worthy, promising, yes, good human being, and that gives me hope.

# Faith Asks for a Teacher

**JOHN ROSENBERG**

John Rosenberg retired from BYU in 2022 where he taught and served in multiple administrative assignments for nearly four decades.

Having been counseled by a patriarch to resist "ideologies of men" that might weaken my testimony of the gospel, my years of graduate training in Upstate New York were a time of tentative embraces: excitement generated by novel theories and wondrous books, balanced by retreats—often anxious and urgent—to the Book of Mormon to reconnect with youthful covenants. In that setting, midway between Palmyra and the Susquehanna, the writings of Eugene England were often the topic for discussion in gatherings of Latter-day Saint graduate students. We shared *Dialogue* essays with one another and debated questions that for me had never been questions. I was nearing the conclusion of my studies when *Dialogues with Myself* was released. Reading it with deep interest, I admired Gene's erudition, his gifts of expression, and his ability to apply the critical tools of his academic discipline to the gospel. I admired what at the time impressed me as his edginess: his willingness to root around in forbidden places and to ask discomfiting questions—questions that by this time I had learned to ask for myself.

Shortly thereafter I packed up my Cervantes and Foucault and England and headed to BYU where I would spend the next four decades. Gene and I were not in the same department, but we were in the same college (Humanities). I knew him better than he knew me, and I continued to read his work ("Easter Weekend" touched me as few essays have), attend his lectures, and follow his service on and off campus. I sat next to him at the English Department banquet where he delivered what I believe was his last address as a BYU employee ("I Just Work Here") and had the opportunity to express my personal admiration for his work and appreciation for his moral example.

When I was invited to contribute to this collection, I decided to return to *Dialogues with Myself*, having not turned its pages since 1984. At that time, I was beginning my career; this time I was ending it. In that sense, the collection bracketed my professional life. It was in the rereading that I discovered how much I had changed—how much Gene had changed for me in those pages. Gone were the edginess and irreverence that I *thought* I had seen years ago. In its place I found a witness that speaks to me with particular and potent resonance and speaks to our time, a time when the "ideologies of men" often entice more than Lehi's wholesome fruit.

In "The Mormon Cross," a meditation on the practice of withholding priesthood and temple blessings to Blacks (written before the 1978 revelation), Gene spoke for those who felt burdened or embarrassed by the practice. And yet:

> I have felt a witness within the deepest core of my being that God lives, that his son Jesus Christ is truly our Savior and has restored his gospel through the Prophet Joseph Smith and maintained his true Church on earth down to his present Prophet. (122)

There it is: not a *resolution* of the burden but a *determination* to hold fast to the witness he had in the absence of witnesses he sought. Later in that same essay he expounded on his method: "I can rationally hope for a change without in any sense implying a challenge to the authority of the Prophet, *whom I sustain with all my heart*" (130). Gene's response is a pattern not just for the controversies of the sixties, but also for those of today and for the unknown ones of tomorrow. Gene somehow channeled my patriarch by reminding me of the syntax of seeking. Successful disciples, including intellectuals buoyed by the salient ideas of ideological waters, put "their faith in the Lord and loyalty to the church *over everything*" (59). The "first principle for Mormon intellectuals," Gene reminds us, is the imperative to "know and use your own great intellectual traditions and the resources of your own true religion *before* you get too impressed with great books and great ideas from other sources" (73). For those of us whose vocation is to teach the young, there is safety in that syntax, for them and for us.

In the 1966 essay on the Atonement—one that for some has been healing and for others heretical—inside the thicket of medieval theology and the rewriting of modern expectations, Gene proposes this simple question about Gethsemane: "If God can have this kind of love for me, who am I to withhold it from myself" (91)? Reading this in 2022, at a time when I experienced the mystery of being generously loved by many without feeling particularly loveable, I nearly jumped from my chair in response to Gene's question. Who am I, indeed? Later in "What It Means to Be a Mormon Christian" he insists, "We recognize that the experience of Atonement with Christ through his grace and through our response is not so much a matter of theology as experience" (180). There is much about the mechanism of Atonement that is unrevealed. Perhaps the reason for revelatory lacunae is that otherwise we might be complacent with an intellectually satisfying explanation and stop questing for the healing experience.

Some time ago in a gospel doctrine class, a member commented that the church isn't true, but the gospel is. It was a muddled way of making the point that the church is an organization composed of inevitably flawed people whose decisions and actions reflect both their goodness and their human limitations. The gospel, meanwhile, is perfect in eternal principles. However, even when the church in its reassuring Ephesian nature (4.11) seems inseparable from its corporate bureaucracy, Gene taught us to never lose faith that the church "is the means the Lord has given us to struggle with the great moral and spiritual imperatives from God for attaining the possible Godhood within us" (48). *Struggle*, even if the contest makes us "halt" (Gen. 32.31).

Those who knew Gene and those who have pondered Terryl Givens's biography know something of the *agon* that motivated Gene's best writing and service. If the wrestling made him halt, that was the price to be paid to grapple with those few things that are transcendent and eternal: the few things that matter. Of that reality Gene confessed, "Reality is too demanding for me to feel very safe anymore in the appalling luxury of my moments of utter skepticism" (204). Skepticism is a challenge; faith is an invitation. Skepticism asks for proof; faith asks for a teacher; skepticism is nourished by pride; faith is nourished by trust. Forty years later, *Dialogues with Myself* has made me more responsive, more teachable and more trusting.

# Recollections of Gene England

**BRENT RUSHFORTH**

Brent Rushforth served a mission in Berlin as the Berlin Wall was being built and was at Stanford with Gene at *Dialogue*'s creation. As a trial lawyer, he stopped oil drilling on Santa Monica, California, beaches, prosecuted Amazon activist Dorothy Stang's murderers in Brazil, and for fifteen years successfully represented prisoners at Guantanamo.

I first met Gene and Charlotte in the fall of 1963 when I returned to Stanford from Berlin where I had served a mission that had stretched to three years. It was love at first sight. They were an arresting couple, young, vibrant, and obviously in love. They presented a whole new world of possibilities to someone just emerging from the cocoon of missionary life.

My three years in Berlin had been an awakening for a kid from Kaysville, Utah, by way of Palo Alto and Stanford. I had watched the Berlin Wall go up, cutting overnight thirty miles through the center of the city, and experienced the violent clash of the two worlds it represented. I had been part of the throng of two million Berliners who swarmed into the streets to witness President Kennedy's triumphant visit to the city celebrating its defiance of Soviet aggression. I had heard Spencer W. Kimball declare during his visit that Berlin would remain free so long as the Lord kept his missionaries there, thus giving our service a heroic ring. And I had experienced an Alma-like conversion regarding the truth of the restored gospel.

But by the fall of 1963, I was coming face to face with the enormous tension of leaving the world of faith and spirituality and reentering the world of doubt and skepticism and the rational mind. This was my pre-mission world and I felt comfortable in it. But I also felt a need to reconcile it with the world of the spirit. It was in building the bridge between these two seemingly irreconcilable worlds that Gene became my indispensable guide. I last saw Gene a couple of days before his death on August 17, 2001. As we reminisced, I told him that I loved him and that he had saved my spiritual life by showing the way to marry the rational mind with all its doubt and skepticism to the world of faith. He had shown me by his life how to walk carefully across the chasm that separates the two.

Our conversation as Gene lay on his deathbed was, inevitably, tender and heartbreakingly difficult. Gene knew he did not have long. He spoke lovingly and movingly of Charlotte and their children. He asked me to watch out for them after his death, a request I left, to my regret, unfulfilled. I told Gene I believed he had influenced thousands, perhaps even millions, of Mormons in the same way his life had powerfully affected my own.

I spoke of three ways in which Gene had proved to be such a powerful force for good in the Mormon world. First was the creation of *Dialogue*. While many, including myself, were present at the creation, Gene was undoubtedly the first mover. It was he who drafted its manifesto and delivered it in an address at Stanford on September 30, 1966. Gene spoke of his optimism regarding Mormonism:

> At least about the future, because I [had] faith that I and many others I knew could help make that future; that the freedom that exists in our religion and in our culture is determined essentially by how willing we are to create it, and that faith was and is based on familiarity with the great resources in Mormon belief to support freedom of inquiry and the process of dialogue as an essential pathway to understanding the universe and the beings in it and in the developing of love between them.

Six decades later, and in spite of attacks from the powerful anti-intellectual tradition of the church, I still share that optimism. I trace its roots to Gene. *Dialogue* in my view remains one of the seminal fruits of and protectors of the Mormon intellectual tradition. Gene was its inspiration and creator.

The second and related of Gene's contributions to my spiritual survival and that of countless others are his essays and books. Without a doubt, the two "Mormon" essays that have most influenced my life are both Gene's. The first is his essay on the Atonement, published in one of the early volumes of *Dialogue*. Its main thesis, that the power at the heart of the Atonement is Christ's power to communicate to an individual's heart his unconditional love, provides the means for her to love herself, forgive herself, and free herself to live a different life. That is the gist of the matter, as Alma's experience shows. His guilt and self-loathing had paralyzed him. When his tortured mind remembered Christ and the Atonement, and before he had done the heavy lifting of any real repentance, its power was shocking to him. It freed him to love himself, forgive himself, and change the course of his life.

The truth of Gene's insight was made powerfully clear to me on a cold winter's night in Berlin: when I took the leap of faith, reaching out to the Lord, and before any repentance, his love for me was communicated instantly and shockingly. Six decades full of life's vicissitudes later, the power of that moment is fresh and new. I attribute my best understanding of what happened to me that night to Gene's teachings of the Atonement.

The second of Gene's essays that has greatly affected my life is his "The Church is as True as the Gospel." Its primary idea is that the structure of the church in putting us together in a framework of mutual caring and service is as important to our learning how to love one another (an essential goal of our mortality) as are the concepts and ideas of our religion. Gene's essay has helped me many times to overcome serious frustrations and disappointments in dealing with church members who hold political, intellectual, and social views different from my own. It has become even more important in the last few years of toxic political divisiveness.

Third, Gene's sometimes more, sometimes less successful struggle to maintain respect and reverence for the priesthood hierarchy of the church while maintaining his fierce independence of thought has helped me face that same challenge. Gene once showed me a letter in which an apostle of the church maintained that it was his responsibility to do the thinking about church doctrine while Gene's responsibility was to do the obeying. I was shocked in the moment, and I am shocked now as I look back on it. I cannot think of a formulation more antithetical to the central concept of our religion and the purpose of our mortal life: to learn and grow by exercising all the God-given powers of our mind, heart, spirit, and body. A moment of truth came for me when a group of us were asked by "the Brethren" (never specifically identified), as the then editors of *Dialogue*, not to publish Lester Busch's now famous world- and church-changing article on Blacks and the priesthood. Looking back on that moment, I think of Gene's lifelong example, sometimes at great personal cost, of maintaining his intellectual and moral independence.

Thank you, Gene. I love you.

# Bearing Testimony Was What Gene Did His Whole Life

**KATHRYN SHIRTS**

Kathryn H. Shirts holds a master's degree from Harvard Divinity School. Her recent research has focused on the historical development of the priesthood/motherhood model and the ideal of Zion as an inclusive community. Like her mentor, Gene England, she was privileged to teach LDS Institute classes, in her case while serving a church education mission in Raleigh, North Carolina, with her husband, Randy.

I knew about Eugene England even before I came to Stanford as a freshman in the fall of 1966. One of my best friends had a copy of the first issue of *Dialogue: A Journal of Mormon Thought*—her parents must have subscribed—and as we sat on her bed sharing our college plans, we talked about how exciting it was that I would be going to the place where *Dialogue* was based. I wanted to meet Gene England.

Arriving in Palo Alto, I found the Stanford student ward a welcome respite from dorm life and the struggle to succeed academically. I looked forward to Sundays like I never had before. There were friends in the ward I could easily relate to, and our adult leaders were supportive. As I became aware of the moral and political concerns swirling around the Stanford campus, however, I realized how distant those concerns were from my experience at church.

The two most pressing social justice issues in 1960s America were civil rights and the war in Vietnam. The national focus on civil rights called attention to any form of discrimination, highlighting the Latter-day Saint policy that Black men could not be ordained to the priesthood and that people of African ancestry could not participate in temple ordinances. Students from universities in the Western Athletic Conference picketed BYU athletic events because of the policy, and Stanford refused to play BYU in any sport. During the height of public unrest about the war in Vietnam, protests also rocked the Stanford campus. I attended seminars on the origins of the war and mass meetings in Memorial Auditorium. Students and non-students patrolled campus encouraging us to boycott classes, and I dodged tear gas more than once on my way home from the library.

Although our adult ward leaders were available and caring, they never probed the issues that were increasingly urgent to us as students. Gene England was the exception. Those of us in his Institute classes (often held at the England home with young children dashing about) discovered we weren't alone in facing the difficult issues of our generation: Gene was willing to discuss our vexing questions because he was wrestling with them himself. He had been concerned about restrictions on Black members of the church long before we were, and he was passionately interested in addressing them. Several of the young men in our student ward were torn between their desire to protest a war they felt was immoral and Elder Boyd K. Packer's condemnation of conscientious objectors. Gene was willing to advise them, even when there was pushback from parents and local leaders about his support.

The high school friend who introduced me to *Dialogue*, one of the most thoughtful and sensitive people I know, felt she could not stay in a church that practiced racial discrimination. Because of Gene, my fellow students and I knew the gospel of Jesus Christ that grounded us spiritually could also inspire us to work for a more just and compassionate world.

I went on to graduate school, married, started a family, and eventually returned to Salt Lake City where my husband was offered a faculty position at the University of Utah. Returning to Utah gave me greater access to the places where people gathered to discuss and debate church history and anything else related to the Latter-day Saint experience. I could hardly wait for summer conferences like the Mormon History Association and the Sunstone Symposium that combined spiritual and intellectual nourishment with the willingness to tackle challenging topics. Gene England was among the speakers I most looked forward to hearing, and, again, I saw him approach difficult issues with both faith and intellectual integrity.

Some church members viewed Gene's ideas with suspicion, but one of the things I admired most about Gene was the way he navigated differences of opinion. First, he advised us to get to know people and let them get to know you as fellow Saints engaged in the hard but rewarding work of building the Kingdom of God on earth. Then, he argued, when people see your commitment to the gospel and know that you truly care about them and their opinions, you can share your own perspectives, enter into dialogue, and remain friends.

I was at the August 1992 Sunstone session where Lavina Fielding Anderson detailed the activities of a committee that was monitoring the publications of scholars for controversial views and sending underlined copies to their local leaders. I remember Gene standing up to condemn such activities without realizing that there were General Authorities on the committee, and then apologizing because of his respect for ecclesiastical authority. At first, Gene seemed as confused as the rest of us about how to respond to the investigations, but he was willing to look for signs of hope and reconciliation. At a later meeting, he shared the example of leaders in one stake who were asked to interview a scholar about his publications. Instead of restricting or chastising him, they joined in giving him a blessing for his research and writing. I was deeply touched by this—it reminded me that redemptive choices are always possible when we listen to each other and to the Spirit.

Nine years later, far too soon, when we filled the Provo Tabernacle at Gene's funeral, I was impressed by the tributes from a few among the multitude of his friends and admirers. But what I remember most was the unusual decision by his stake president, James Toronto, to conclude the funeral with an audio recording of Gene giving his own testimony. Hearing his words one last time, I realized that bearing testimony was what Gene had been doing all his life. He acted on what he believed in. He recognized that skirting difficult issues does not build faith. He understood that true faith is the willingness to look honestly at our failings as individuals and as a community, while at the same time believing God can lift us to a holier and more inclusive place when we seek his guidance in patience and charity. Many people have inspired me, but Gene is one of the few who has truly shaped the way I see the world and showed me how to chart my path.

# The Kindness of Gene and Charlotte

## HELEN CLAIRE SIEVERS

Helen Claire Sievers, a "jack of all trades, and master of none" has been a hospital administrator, a Jesuit high school principal, and a community court judge in the Marshall Islands. She served as the executive director of World-Teach, and the New England Conservatory's "El Sistema" program, as well as the academic dean of the Asian University for Women in Bangladesh. In addition, she has taught astronomy at Wellesley and Bentley Colleges. A native of Washington, DC, she has lived mainly in the Boston area with her husband, LeRoy, and their five children.

In the summer of 1997, my friend, Francine Bennion, and I went to Europe. We rented a car and were doing the usual tourist routes, beginning in London. Because Francine was good friends with Gene and Charlotte England, they invited us to stay with them while we were in London, where Gene was running the summer theatre program for BYU. I had met the Englands before but didn't know them very well. I deeply respected what Gene had done in founding *Dialogue* and knew how widely admired he was teaching at the Y, and I had eaten at Charlotte's ice cream shop in Provo. What I didn't know was what incredibly generous, selfless, and kind people they were. They didn't just let us stay with them, which was such a gift already, because hotels in London were pricey, but both of them made sure we did and saw the best of the city.

Gene didn't just tell us what he recommended we not miss, but took us himself to the British Museum, the National Gallery, and the Tate. And at each we got the most incredible personal tour, with Gene literally running between the things at each that we just "couldn't miss," our own personalized private tour. He took us to the theatre and made sure we saw the best plays, since that's what he was there to do with his students. He knew all the plays well, which was especially helpful. I was astonished at his energy and determination that we had the best possible experiences in London. And we certainly did. But that wasn't all! While we were there, my daughter, Sara, contacted me to say she would be in London the next day. Charlotte and Gene insisted she stay with them as well, even though their apartment was small, and Francine and I were already stretching it. They borrowed a cot and made room for Sara too and made her feel as welcome as old friends. Such warmth, such inclusion, such kindness I have rarely seen. I knew of Gene's intellect, but I saw firsthand his profound goodness to ordinary people.

So, when Gene became ill a few years later, I was coming from our home in the Boston area to visit my mother in Provo, and, remembering his immense kindness to me a few years before, I wanted to do something, anything, for him. Because Gene and Charlotte had lived in Massachusetts for a few years while Gene was in school, I thought Gene might enjoy a real Boston lobster dinner, for old times. So, I brought on the airplane with me the cooked lobster, clams, corn, and dessert! I'm not sure if Gene felt like eating, but even in his illness he was his same warm, generous, outgoing self, and I was happy to have had the chance to try to do something for this wonderful man who had been so kind to me, my daughter, and our mutual friend.

# Cousins Forever

**JERRY AND KRIS STURGILL**

Jerry and Kris Sturgill live in Boise, Idaho. Jerry has served as a board member for various educational, conservation, and humanitarian organizations. Kris is a community activist as a donor, volunteer, and board member for various humanitarian organizations, including the Wassmuth Human Rights Education Center, the International Rescue Committee, The Women's and Children's Alliance (a shelter for battered women and children), and the Interfaith Sanctuary (the only low-barrier homeless shelter in Boise for individuals and families).

Of the many fortuities of our lives, our connection to Gene and Charlotte England may be our most fortunate. For me, it took about twenty years to get rolling. Kris was aboard much sooner. Here's the story.

Eugene England and my father, also named "Eugene," are first cousins. They and I descended from the daughters of Jacob Hartvigsen, a salty Norwegian farmer from southeastern Idaho.

Before college, I had heard about but never met this cousin of my father. I had only heard the family gossip and so was vaguely aware of a "Mormon intellectual" in the family who had started a controversial, non-church-sanctioned publication (gasp!) at Stanford University.

In the cocoon of my childhood, I had never stepped outside our insular church community, met a person of color, or confronted racism, feminism, same-gender attraction, the anti-war movement, or any of the other issues I would later learn were concerns for Gene and Charlotte.

Thus, I was pretty naïve and innocent, although happy as I loaded up my first car (a jacked-up Ford Fairlane with a memorable hole in the floorboard purchased from an uncle for $200) and drove from Twin Falls, Idaho to my first year at BYU.

After a solid first year in the honors program, a foreign mission, and a summer as a professional guide on the whitewater rivers of Idaho, I met my future wife, a co-ed in a miniskirt named Kris, who had just arrived at BYU from the San Francisco Bay Area.

After months of dating, she invited me to Thanksgiving dinner with her family, who had recently moved back to Utah from out east ("out east" meaning everywhere beyond Denver). Kris's father's first cousin, Charlotte, had asked her to come to dinner and bring a date.

We drove north from Utah Valley, knocked on the door of an attractive prairie-style house, and were greeted by Charlotte, who swept us into a house full of warmth, Thanksgiving smells, and kids to meet her husband, Gene. In the "get to know me" conversation that followed, the double genealogical coincidences were revealed and celebrated. I had finally met my famous, infamous relative!

Filled with dinner and discussion, we drove back to Provo, my mind spinning. There was a sparkle of pride in Kris's and my newly discovered family heritages and more twinges of attraction to this young woman from the Bay Area who, with her family, had regularly visited the England home in Palo Alto when Gene was a student at Stanford.

Dating and marriage would follow, as the England household, relocated to Provo, became an epicenter of our BYU experience. This included helping Gene gather loads of bricks from demolished old buildings, working as an unpaid hod carrier, and hanging sheet rock in the self-designed and built pioneer-style homestead on Andrus Lane, just north of the BYU campus.

As a student, I made regular visits to Gene's office to ask for help with my writing (it was pretty bad), and Kris and I often visited Andrus Lane. We received frequent, open invitations to the still-being-finished house for family meals, discussions, lectures, recitals, and other marvelous experiences.

I became an English major and strove to follow Gene's example—and still do—although I eventually defaulted to law school. I soaked up his writing (which took a lot of catching up); collected and consumed past issues of *Dialogue* from used bookstores; subscribed to it and *Sunstone Magazine*; and collected autographed copies of Gene's books to add to a growing collection of autographed Wallace Stegner first editions (but that's another story).

I often threw myself on Gene's good will and family relationship. He listened and counseled patiently to help me through youthful faith crises—as he did for so many young members of the church—sometimes at his office in the English Department and more often in sessions at Andrus Lane. Toward the end of our time in "Happy Valley," I could sense his own angst (but never anger, to me at least) about the abusive "othering" of "Mormon intellectuals" by certain senior members of church leadership.

I lament the torment imposed on this faithful, Christlike man, and still struggle with how to bring his and my own personal experience, study, and faith into synchrony with church doctrine and leadership (or at least reduce such dissonance). Thankfully, I have managed through it all with the epistemological and theological perspectives and strategies taught by Cousin Gene and his example of courage—to doubt, to question, and to seek dialogue. So far, so good.

With Gene and Charlotte as our examples, Kris and I have maintained our faith and activity and have had sublime experiences in the church and beyond it—like Gene and Charlotte, keeping our doors and hearts open to neighbors, friends and strangers, straights and gays, believers and nonbelievers.

We practice the Englands' example of eagerness to cross social and cultural boundaries to welcome (and to be welcomed by) members of other faith communities and community organizations, and to join arm in arm with them for humanitarian purposes—like promoting human rights, helping refugees, solving homelessness, and supporting Pride.

Following Gene's example as an educator and church leader, I have in my own teaching and leadership roles listened and counseled in situations where faith has been shaken by history and doctrine—cases hard to reconcile with the Second Great Commandment—and most recently with our LGBTQ+ brothers and sisters, and with their families and friends.

In summary, much of the good we have tried to do in our lives finds original inspiration and purpose in our connection to Gene and Charlotte—not to mention our good luck as sprouts from their same family trees. Their love and attention to us young newlyweds at BYU (together with Charlotte's cinnamon rolls) kept us upright, gave us needed courage for the future, and inspired us to live lives of compassion, service, and faith.

# Expanding the Borders of the Mold

**JENEE WALLACE**

Jenee Wallace is busier than ever now that she has "retired"—communication director for the San Diego North Stake, principal second in the Tifereth Israel Community Orchestra, vice president of her homeowner association, a Tastyworks options trader, and traveling with her husband, Judge J. Clifford Wallace, who at ninety-six is still an active senior judge on the Court of Appeals for the Ninth Circuit, working with him as he has assisted judiciaries in over ninety countries. They share fifteen children with spouses, fifty-four grandchildren with spouses, and over sixty "greats." She confesses that it has become increasingly challenging at ninety-one to remember where she put her iPhone or parked her car, and to remind her husband what day of the week it is.

What does "the mold" look like? Whatever it looks like, as a woman in the Church of Jesus Christ of Latter-day Saints, I didn't fit it. At the same time, the church felt like my home, the place where I belonged. My mother was a strong, opinionated woman who didn't hesitate to tell church leaders how she felt things should be. She spoke her mind and remained one hundred percent committed to the church. My father, on the other hand, was always agreeable, supported everyone, made everyone feel good about him or herself, and never ruffled people's feathers. He rarely spoke his mind, was loved by everyone, and was privately reported to occasionally slip off the straight and narrow, yet remained one hundred percent committed to the church and was three times called as a bishop, at which calling he excelled.

Those two models gave me a great deal of leeway in my personal approach to the gospel. The church felt like the home where I belonged. I married an amazing man, had six spectacular children, and always remained close to my core spiritual beliefs and activities. At this point, however, I found drawn to question whether what I had been taught all my life was the only way. I had never had cause to consider any other spiritual path. I wanted to look at other religions but surely did not want to impede the progress in the LDS Church for either my husband or my children. Consequently, I started quietly and privately looking at other churches, reading other religious books, and meditating, and I attended the Buddhist ashram. I seriously considered *A Course in Miracles*, a series of books written in a manner similar to the way the Book of Mormon was written. I was impressed by how similar its teachings were to the Book of Mormon; however, I knew I felt at home with the Book of Mormon and not with *A Course in Miracles*. But there was that "mold" problem.

It was Eugene England who helped me move toward a feeling of peace about the mold. I vividly remember sitting on a grassy hill somewhere near Stanford University where Gene drew the circle around that "Mormon mold" big and wide enough to draw me within its boundaries. After that conversation, I began, like my mother, to feel comfortable exploring my own feelings, drawing my own conclusions, and, with confidence, voicing my opinions, or, like my father, to agreeably and usually without ruffling feathers, express what seemed right to me. The borders of the mold were bigger and wider than I had thought. And perhaps there really wasn't a mold anyway.

Gene was a model for taking the time to explore, study, and draw one's own conclusions, expanding the borders of the mold. He ruffled more feathers than my mother. He did not learn to follow the agreeable pattern of my father. He generated pain and suffering for himself and for his family. Those of us who consider him a favorite friend and valuable mentor are grateful for the freedom to think for ourselves which he modeled, and we will forever remember that he always remained one hundred percent committed to the Church of Jesus Christ of Latter-day Saints.

# At Rest in the Fluttering Providence of the World

**ROSALYNDE FRANDSEN WELCH**

Rosalynde Frandsen Welch is a research fellow and associate director at the Neal A. Maxwell Institute for Religious Scholarship. She earned a BA in English from Brigham Young University, where she studied Shakespeare and Latter-day Saint literature under Eugene England. She earned a PhD in early modern English literature from the University of California, San Diego, where her dissertation included a chapter on an obscure Shakespeare play that would have amused Gene. Her research now focuses on Latter-day Saint scripture and theology, and in this, Gene's valued influence is evident.

In June of 1994, strawberries were ripening in Kent and Pete Sampras was competing at Wimbledon. Spectators thronged the District line en route to the grassy courts, Eugene England among the crowd with a gaggle of BYU students in tow. Gene loved tennis, he loved the Tube, and he loved sharing his bounding enthusiasms with any willing accomplice.

It was late in the term, and we were used to his ways. This was an impromptu excursion, and, typically, the group was short a ticket. This deterred Gene not at all, whose trust in the providence of London was Edenic. An extra ticket could always be rummaged up from a friendly house manager or a late patron. This time, though, Gene's charisma and patience at the box office could not produce the magic slip allowing entrance to the court complex.

Refusing defeat, Gene conferred with his students outside the gates when he noticed a faint fluttering behind the bleachers. A white scrap, fair as a rose and innocent as a baby dove, landed just inside the fence. Gene instructed a student to retrieve it through the gapped wire. It was a ticket stub, granting re-entrance to any holder. London once again provided faithfully for the guileless. We feasted on strawberries and cream at Centre Court.

Gene's receptive and trustful way of being in the world was more a practical posture, perhaps a childhood inheritance of his Idaho wheatfields, than an intellectual judgment on how one ought to live. Still, he brought the same stance to the classroom, where he rested in the expectation that both his students and the texts he put before us would open and bring forth meaning. One night he gathered the group, which that spring included myself and my now husband, in the parlor of the Kensington row house where we met for classes. He had planned for us to attend the National Theatre's British premiere of Tony Kushner's *Perestroika*, a transgressive fantasia on Latter-day Saint themes in the context of New York's gay community in the mid-1980s. The play opened, heart-stoppingly, with a tremendous winged angel fluttering over the AIDS-afflicted protagonist, whom she then approached in carnal embrace, called as a prophet, and entrusted with a sacred book. And it just got wilder from there. It was a play likely to befuddle even the self-judged urbane among us.

But Gene had faith in art's capacity to touch truth by "search[ing] into and contemplat[ing] the darkest abyss."[1] And he had equal faith in our reciprocal capacity to redeem the play with attentive interpretation. He quoted Matthew 15:11: "It is not what goes into the mouth that defiles a person, but it is what comes out of the mouth that defiles." We are less likely to be corrupted by the art we take in, he suggested, than by any ugly or divisive interpretive use we might make of it. Conversely, even offensive and polarizing art—if it *is* art—can be redeemed with noble-minded reading that reaches for mercy, forgiveness, and reconciliation.

Mercy, forgiveness, and reconciliation were his every word that spring. His faith in the power of Christian mercy to heal any breach saturated his teaching of *King Lear*, which we attended as a group at the Royal Shakespeare Company early in the term. The curtain opened on a huge map of Lear's realm papering the stage. As his kingdom and family fractured, the map shredded beneath the actors' feet. But the meta-drama orchestrated by Cordelia for the spiritual rescue of her father—"healing theater," Gene called it—overpowered the elemental brutality of the play's end. Cordelia is murdered, Lear dies of grief in the aftermath, and Kent implores the survivors to "Vex not his ghost. O, let him pass!" In the director's staging, the ghost of Cordelia arrives to accompany the ghost of Lear offstage, father and daughter reconciled in death to "live, and pray, and sing, and tell old tales, and laugh at gilded butterflies" (Act 5, Scene 3, 12–14). Gene wept over this scene. Christian reconciliation, for him, was no reconciliation at all if it did not bind earth with its heaven, life with its death, flesh with its wing.

Unusually, Gene's trust in a spiritual otherworld seemed only to hone his appetite for this world, of which his London was surely the premiere microcosm. Beauties natural and human, the finest art and entertainment, Indian curries and fish-and-chips: London gave bountifully, and he relished it all, body and spirit. An illuminating line reading of a poem or play brought him the same renewing soul-pleasure. Without sanctimony, Gene brought a quality of attention, specificity, and favor to relationships with his students that I

1. "History, 1838–1856, volume C-1 [2 November 1838–31 July 1842][b]," p. 904[b], The Joseph Smith Papers, accessed Apr. 15, 2022, josephsmithpapers.org.

can only describe as a blessing. Later that spring, he invited me into collaboration as his London teaching assistant for the following year; the year after that, he eased me through an unoriginal MTC faith crisis as patiently as he might have Matthew Arnold on Dover Beach. He drove to Manti and toasted John and me at our wedding breakfast in 1998, the last time I saw him alive. He did this kind of thing, and more, for scores of students, but somehow we felt singularly cherished. My best explanation for this effect is that his Mormonism taught him to approach relationship as a spiritual practice.

He's been gone a long time now, and I am not one who sees ghosts crossing on and offstage. I am unlike Gene in that way, I think. Nor am I blessed with his Edenic confidence, his rest in the world's good providence. But I have my moments. Several years ago, my Shakespeare-obsessed fourteen-year-old was aflame to see the National Theatre's filmed production of Hamlet, which was screening at a local art cinema. It starred Benedict Cumberbatch, and I did not account for his celebrity appeal in estimating the demand for tickets. When we arrived, the box office line already stretched down the block. We gamely queued up and crossed our fingers. When the box office agent sold the last ticket to the woman immediately ahead of us, disappointment got the best of Elena, and she wept bitter tears.

I remembered Gene then, and the fluttering behind the Wimbledon bleachers. I told her we would hang around a few more minutes and see if anything turned up. Minutes ticked by, and the start time came and went. Elena had bravely faced her grief and was reconciled to leaving, when I saw a man approaching with a familiar purpose in his step.

"Would you happen to need a ticket to the movie?" he asked. "I've got an extra."

Elena made it to her seat before the previews ended. As a lifelong Mormon I don't often pray to saints, but there on the sidewalk I offered up a benediction to Gene, fair as a rose and innocent as a dove.

# Rejoicing with Gene in Heaven

**WARNER WOODWORTH**

Warner Woodworth is a global social entrepreneur combating poverty through his forty-one NGOs in sixty-two countries. He is author of twelve books and three-hundred-plus articles. He holds an MA and PhD in organizational behavior from the University of Michigan, Ann Arbor. A professor of management at BYU for forty years, he now teaches a University of Utah course, "How to Change the World."

I don't recall exactly when I first met Gene England, but it was a blessing in my life from that point forward. He was in the College of Humanities at BYU, and I was in the Marriott School of Management. Nevertheless, our paths crossed on campus from time to time. Once, when I was speaking at Oxford, I crashed their pad in London for several days when Gene and Charlotte were running BYU's Study Abroad program. It was a joyful respite from some challenges I was going through back in Utah. Just to sit on the couch with the two of them exchanging ideas and sharing experiences was refreshing, even healing for me. Of course, they invited me to travel with them and their students to a Shakespeare play and other cultural events, which few business professors have the chance to enjoy. This is just one example of the Englands' love, thoughtfulness, and generosity blessing my life.

For years Gene and I both served as bishopric first counselors in our respective wards in the same Pleasant View chapel near the MTC. We would often encounter one another, not only at stake priesthood leadership meetings, firesides, and other gatherings, but also in the halls of the ward house. Exchanging pleasantries, occasionally bemoaning bureaucratic aspects of the church and our responsibilities, respectively, we always enjoyed such encounters.

Over the years, my wife, Kaye, and I have been guests at various gatherings in the beautiful England home adjacent to the BYU campus where some of the best and brightest LDS thinkers and scholars, as well as common Saints, have met to explore the meaning of life, engage in political discourse, and, of course, discuss Mormonism with brilliant insights. I'm grateful Charlotte has continued that tradition.

In the 1980s as an advocate of worker empowerment in the US and throughout the world, I began working with Lech Walesa and other Solidarity officers in Poland who suffered under fascist controls of the USSR in Moscow and the Polish government in Warsaw. In those early years, Lech was under house arrest, but I was able to meet with and advise him and other union leaders. I was also successful in bringing several of them to BYU, where we held huge speaking events about the problems of democracy under the military dictatorship based in Warsaw. It was during this time that, because of his big heart and gospel understanding, Gene was inspired to launch the Food for Poland program, a local Utah effort to raise funds to get powdered milk for the children in Poland during the Soviet oppression. It was a huge success, which I was pleased to support.

Following my efforts to establish worker ownership and industrial democracy across the U.S. and beyond, I next focused on what became the major thrust of my last forty years—empowering the poor in sixty-two developing nations by establishing NGOs based in the US (most of them in Utah with Latter-day Saint colleagues). This work is chronicled in my recent book, *Radiant Mormonism: Using Our Faith in Christ to Power World-changing Service* (By Common Consent Press, 2022).

After Gene joined the faculty at Utah Valley State University (formerly UVSC, now Utah Valley University), he and I reconnected, and I was honored when he invited me to receive the Award for Humanitarian Service presented by UVSU's Program in Religious Studies at its Center for the Study of Ethics. At that event, my good friend, Elder Marion D. (Duff) Hanks, was the speaker. He and I had been serving for a decade on the board of a growing NGO I started in the Philippines called Enterprise Mentors International. I appreciated the recognition because it opened doors for me to begin mobilizing UVSU students to join students from BYU I had recruited over the previous decade to participate in the various humanitarian programs I helped organize around the world. It was a joyous occasion to be there when, in the spirit of Gene's life, Elder Hanks spoke of love, justice, and the humanitarian spirit of Mormonism.

I rejoice in having known Eugene England from the time he launched *Dialogue* in the 1960s. Although I was younger than him, we shared the same passion for the intellect, deep Latter-day Saint values, expansive views of eternity, and harmonizing the mind and the Holy Spirit in our lives. I don't know how Gene was able to launch that amazing journal and contribute to the origins and growth of *Sunstone*, both critical publications for the Latter-day Saint community. He had a knack for seizing opportunities to enlighten young Latter-day Saints and talked often about the great philosophers of the church: Parley P. Pratt, James E. Talmage, B. H. Roberts, John E. Widtsoe, Lowell E. Bennion, Neal Maxwell, and others. He was also able to foster dialogues with critics of the church, including some University of

Utah professors who criticized the Brethren and the teachings of Mormonism. At the same time, Gene was on the faculty of the Institute of Religion at the University of Utah, opening students' minds by exploring the intellectual challenges of Latter-day Saint doctrine, policy, and philosophy. In doing so, he worked with two other of his and my heroes, T. Edgar Lyon and Lowell Bennion, both of whom were my mentors as a young college student.

Through his formal and informal teaching, Gene was successful in opening Latter-day Saint college students' minds by helping them explore the expanse of heaven while wrestling with the tensions between the mind and the heart and between the mental and the spiritual elements of Mormonism. I fully believe his life's work helped keep many young Latter-day Saints from leaving the church because, through him, they were able to see that the mind can be integrated with the spirit in an authentic, purposeful life.

Gene helped me appreciate the fact that intellectual Latter-day Saint scholarship is not just a way for students to remain faithful but is a necessary element in the survival and growth of Mormonism itself. We both have had many friends and loved ones leave the church, criticize the Brethren, and ridicule those who stay faithful. But Gene's life demonstrates that one can be a faithful disciple of Christ while pursuing the rigors of intellectual and spiritual inquiry without ignoring historical reality.

I mention a final, personal experience that happened when I visited Gene during his last days in Utah Valley Hospital. Even though he was getting quite weak physically, his mind was clear, and we had a deep and meaningful exchange of ideas about life, death, truth, and eternity. As I got up to leave, he asked me for a hug. As we embraced one another, he kissed me on the cheek and requested I do the same to him in the spirit of the Savior kissing the men and women he closely loved. A few days later Gene passed away. I was but one of the thousands who attended his glorious funeral in the old Provo pioneer tabernacle, a structure that both my wife's and my ancestors helped build in the 1800s. It is fitting that such a building is now a temple.

# The Next Dance

**CHARLOTTE ENGLAND**

Charlotte England is a musician, artist, writer, and legendary hostess of vibrant dialogues. She and her husband, Gene, worked side by side in many important enterprises, including serving a mission to Samoa in their early twenties, launching *Dialogue: A Journal of Mormon Thought* while in graduate school at Stanford (during which she nurtured their six children), taking part in study abroad and theater courses in London, gathering food as part of Food for Poland, and building a large home near the BYU campus that for half a century has been a retreat, shelter, and refuge for thousands—and remains so today. Charlotte is still living her "good life" as she begins her nineties.

It was a beautiful fall day in 1952, the kind that you feel good things could happen on, or was it wishful thinking, having just worked my last day at Hill Air Force Base as a riveter? Not the greatest environment, but I was earning enough to cover tuition and most costs for my freshman year at the University of Utah. I was in my bedroom anticipating the classes I had registered for and trimming my hair with a double-edged razor. It saved me $1.25, the cost of a hairdresser. I messed up sometimes, but my natural curl covered mistakes. Then the phone rang.

There was no one else home, so I ran up the basement stairs two at a time and, just slightly breathless, grabbed the receiver, and gave a cheery "Hello." Gene England's familiar voice responded, "Hi, Charlotte."

When I was dating Gene's best friend, Floyd, we often went on double dates with Gene and whatever popular girl he was dating at the time. We would often go dancing, the four of us, and sometimes during the dance, switched partners. Dancing with Gene was an unpredictable experience. He knew how to surprise you with a little extra turn to the foxtrot step. We had all been good friends at East High School in Salt Lake City, but Gene and his friends had graduated a year before me, and I hadn't heard from them since, so I was a little puzzled by the call, but there was no hesitancy in Gene's voice when he said, "I'd like to take you to the Hello Dance at the U next week." I laughed because I felt a little excited but also concerned, wondering if this might be a joke. I had thought of Gene more as a close relative than as someone to date. He assured me the invitation was for real. He wanted to go on a date *with me.*

The dance, to welcome the incoming freshmen, followed a week of activities on campus that I had missed, having worked almost up to the day classes would start. I accepted the invitation and asked what people would be wearing. He said casual dress. So, I assumed that a home-sewn, moss-green corduroy skirt and white cotton shirt, plus my saddle oxfords with ankle socks, would fit the bill, but I remained a little puzzled during the days leading up to the dance. What would it be like to be on a date with Gene?

When the evening came, I could hear my mother from my bedroom below, answering the pound of the brass lion head on our front door. I left my room and started up the basement stairs, this time not two at a time, still a little unsure. I heard "The Third Man Theme" being played on our Kimball upright piano. Over the next year, this melody became Gene's way of letting me know he was there and waiting. I ended up connecting the song more with Gene than with Orson Welles. But seeing him playing it then made me pause to think how at ease he was in our home. But I was still feeling a little nervous about how this evening would go.

On our way to campus, we drove in his parents' Oldsmobile down Harrison Avenue to 13th East. Gene seemed at ease with the two of us in the front seat without other dates. I may have made a comment about that, but he responded with something about liking it this way. We probably talked about how we had spent our summer. He worked on his family's wheat farm in Idaho and seemed genuinely interested in my first and only attempt at picking pie cherries in brambling scratchy branches, then on to riveting airplane wings. I asked if he didn't get lonely on the farm, driving a tractor all day through acres of wheat. He said he did a lot of thinking and that helped break the monotony. Also, writing letters kept him in touch with friends. I found some of those letters while sorting his papers that went to the Marriott Library at the U.

We were one of the first to arrive at the Student Union building. The evening was gently cool as we walked up the front steps. Inside, the rich red carpet and brass railings caught my eye. The ballroom was empty except for the band setting up on the small stage. Gene didn't seem surprised that the musicians and we were the only ones on the dance floor. He took my hand as we walked across the room. "Come on. I'll show you the view from the balcony." I was trying to take all this in—the ballroom, the view, and Gene. It was beginning to get dark, and we could see the city lights just coming on. I was feeling more at ease, even really comfortable to be standing there next to him. I was seeing him in a different way. The band started warming up with a familiar song. "Let's dance." Gene took my hand and led me to the empty dance floor that seemed immense with just the two of us dancing. It felt a little strange at first, but soon I began to enjoy having the entire space and band to ourselves. Gene was a good dancer and slipped in some tricky little steps, but I followed with surprising ease.

As others started arriving, I recognized my high school friends and could see they had really dressed up for the occasion. I learned it was Rush Week, so they were showing off their best, hoping to be selected by one of the sororities on campus. And there we were—Gene in his short-sleeved Stradivari shirt and casual slacks and me in my homemade cords and shirt. I felt like a round peg in a square hole. I clearly didn't belong there. I was mortified and whispered to Gene, "I think we should leave." But if Gene was embarrassed, it didn't show. He said, "Just a few more times around the floor, then see if you want to leave."

So, we danced again and again and didn't leave. A photographer for the *Utonian*, the school yearbook, came up to us to ask if he could take our picture. "You two look like you're having so much fun." By that time, I was not only having fun but was very comfortable with Gene. We had danced our way into our own world where everything felt natural between us.

So began our courtship. We found ourselves using every spare moment between and after classes to be together. Gene even signed up for my music appreciation class with Reid Nibley to spend more time with me, even though his major was math at the time.

So the year went; classes, my part-time job as a file clerk at the State Capitol, Gene editing *The Pen*, a campus periodical, and dancing almost weekly, sometimes at the Saltair pavilion—a great dance floor—the Rainbow Rendezvous when the Mills Brothers performed, and, of course, church dances, during the week sometimes hopping from one ward to another to catch the last minutes before they closed for the evening.

A year later, in September, Gene and I went early to a broadcast of the Mormon Tabernacle Choir on Temple Square. We were walking around the grounds when we came to a low iron fence and gate that led to the area where wedding groups gathered for photos. There were no signs to keep us out, so we went in. It was like a dance, as he gently led me to a spot near the temple where we could see the first rays of sunrise peek over the gray wall that surrounded the temple grounds. That was the moment Gene took my left hand and slipped a diamond ring on my finger. It was an unspoken proposal that wasn't necessary because we both knew what the answer would be. But the ring was still a total surprise. I've always felt self-conscious of my large hands and didn't want to draw attention to them with jewelry, but Gene broke through that and later told me that my hands were the first thing that attracted him to me. Perhaps that's why he perfectly guessed my ring size. The choir performance was kind of a blur that morning as we sat in the glow of what had happened just minutes before.

We had dated for a year, been friends even longer, and by now were engaged. Gene would be leaving for a mission within months when we sought counsel from a man we trusted and admired, Elder Spencer W. Kimball, who at the time gave counsel to young couples before marriage. We were seeking some good advice to our dilemma of getting married before finishing school while Gene served his mission or just waiting for his return. Our conversation with Elder Kimball was warm, delightful, and personal. What a surprise when he gave counsel to us before leaving his office. "I think your first mission is marriage," he said, and added something about everything working out for the good.

We took it to heart and chose the break between fall and winter quarters. I remodeled my older sister's wedding dress, borrowed my best friend's wedding veil, and held the reception in Gene's parents' home. It was low-budget to be sure, but we were happy. We also managed to weave our way through most of the pressures of school and well-intentioned adults' advice on where we should live (thank you, but no, we preferred not to live in his parents' basement to save money) and, fortunately, found an attachment to a house for forty dollars. It was a cinder block structure, a wall heater between the kitchen and bedroom with just enough space for a couch and chair in the small living room. We were even gifted with a box of kittens at our door one rainy day. They were almost our only guests.

With no phone, we relied on the mail, and when a note came from Elder LeGrand Richards to interview Gene for his mission, Elder Richards invited me to come with Gene to the interview. The feeling I had from the thirty minutes or so with Elder Richards was very much like our time with Elder Kimball—very comforting.

We anticipated Gene's call soon after that. But what we didn't anticipate were two thick envelopes addressed to each of us. We had to reread the letters and instructions to make sure of what we had just read. We had both been called to serve two and half years in Samoa. Our lives were about to take a very different turn. We were about to learn some new dance steps.

We sold our car to help cover the forty dollars the mission required each month and borrowed my brother's beat-up car that had a view of the road through a hole in the floor. We managed to move our few belongings to our parents' basements, did the blood tests and shots (a first for me), applied for passports, and studied up on Samoa.

Saying goodbyes to family and friends at the station was an emotional moment, but Brent Eager, a close friend and one of Gene's basketball buddies in the ward, was in our group boarding the train to San Francisco. He entertained all of us with his ukulele. It was a little crowded in the top berth, but Gene and I knew how to make the space work for us. We even managed to kneel for a night prayer. We ate my mom's fried chicken the next morning, which we shared with Brent.

My brother, George, and his wife, LaRue, met us at the station and lined up a dinner for the next evening with Granny Herrick, our adopted grandma who, during WWI, had invited marines, including my father, stationed along the coastal towns of Eureka and Loleta, to their homes—and so became Granny Herrick to us.

She was so gracious and mindful of our situation and made sure we were served Shirley Temple drinks when the other guests had alcohol. The day we boarded the ship, they came out to see us off. As we pulled away from the dock, leaving our family and country behind, I was so grateful that Gene and I were having this new experience together. It's a silly thought, but maybe Elders Richard and Kimball sensed we could do this dance together.

There were about fifteen of us twenty-year-old missionaries on the *SS Oronsay*, an ocean liner that was taking us across the Pacific Ocean to the various countries where we would serve: New Zealand, Australia, and Samoa, the place where Gene and I would serve. Gene and another missionary arranged for us to use the children's playroom on the ship, that was available that hour, for Sunday service. To our delight, we met with Māoris and Samoans who had joined us during our stopover in Hawaii after visiting the Hawaii Temple. Their warmth and loving acceptance were contagious in the Sunday service. Later, their dancing and singing on deck took us into another world, one that would soon be familiar to us.

Another time, when we heard music coming from the dance floor, Gene and I did what came naturally—we danced. It was not meant to last, for in less than a minute, Gene got a tap on his shoulder from one of the traveling missionaries informing us that missionaries weren't allowed to dance, which we didn't know applied to married couples. Nevertheless, we reluctantly conformed and joined the others outside on the deck, but it didn't diminish our enthusiasm for something we loved to do.

We soon learned where that energy would be used. Upon our arrival in Samoa, we were assigned to Vaiola, a small village on the island of Savaii, a larger, more primitive island than Upolu and Tutuila.

After arriving at the coast, we were greeted by Fitisunamu, a very large, lovable police chief. He had arranged for the horses and a teacher from the village to take us to our new place. Our suitcases were dropped into saddlebags that bumped against our legs with each step as our horses plodded their way up the mountain. I felt sorry for the horses, swayed back and tired. I learned later that the grass they eat lacks nutrition because it grows so fast due to the heavy rainfall. But they were getting up the mountain now, and I was grateful for that.

Metaphorically speaking, all those dances we did before our mission served as a training for what was ahead in this new, lush, tropical island, including a new language we would soon learn and people with whom we would fall in love. The work was a bonding experience for us, now six months into our marriage. We were just two people, adapting like missionaries do, without family, schoolmates, or friends, but always aware of the pluses with our situation.

That's one of the challenges missionaries face, and it's compounded if you don't work well with your companion. That wasn't our problem, so we went to work right away to improve things in the house we shared with four elders. One of them served as the school principal. Another, from a farm in Wyoming, was assigned to work with the men in the village to improve the profitability of the coconut plantation and cocoa production, a source of income for some of the families. A third elder was responsible for developing a road from the coast up to the village, anticipating trucks and cars in the future. His main equipment was a large Caterpillar that was always breaking down. His frustration was apparent. Our experiences and expectations as missionaries were varied, which sometimes led to tense moments with all of us living under the same roof.

It was evident that no woman had lived in the old, threadbare, termite-eaten house for some time, if at all. In our shared journal, Gene wrote the following about the house's condition: "Men by themselves seem to forget civilization with vigor." He went on to express his concern that "discouragement sets in on everyone here and they settle into the rut more or less and forget or disregard the fresh ideas and resolutions they had when they came—God help me not to forget, please."

We felt responsible to improve things, so we began with a deep clean and a new layer of white paint in the kitchen. It took a little while for the other missionaries in the house to get used to us making changes, but we kept trying. In the end, it took a crisis to bring a healthy unity to our group when Gene developed a rash and then sores that turned into blood poisoning. I prayed and begged God to spare Gene, to guide me for some way to heal him. As others learned what was happening, they offered to give him a blessing, and, in that moment, I found the words of kindness on his behalf a beautiful and welcome sight and sound. The women in the village were right there offering their own medicinal ointments and salves, for which I was grateful. Not knowing if they would work, I didn't turn any away, counting on God moving in mysterious ways to heal Gene. I continued to bathe his hand where the original infection started. It seemed to soothe him, if nothing else. I kept a steady watch on the red lines from his hand to the top of his arm that gradually faded by the third day. When it looked like he would survive, I was bursting with gratitude to God and those who played any part in his healing. I laid by Gene's side that night, listening to him breathing in his sleep. Tears ran onto my pillow as I whispered to God, as if he were there, "Thank you."

It delighted me when I saw Gene sitting cross-legged on the grass playing Whirly Bird with the Samoan children. He seemed to enjoy it as much as they did. We had dressed their wounds whenever needed and had earned their trust in the process. He also asked his students to help him learn to play cricket. Since Savaii was under the British Commonwealth, someone had the good foresight to build a cricket field in the middle of the village, and Gene found playing cricket was an opportunity to teach good sportsmanship to the young, energetic boys, who sometimes lost their temper over a bad call.

Another opportunity to teach good sportsmanship arose when we were transferred to a village with several young men who wanted to play basketball. Gene ordered a basketball through mission headquarters and encouraged the boys to pitch in to cover costs so they would be responsible for the ball and the backboard they built together. Gene was a good leader with young people. I think these experiences influenced him to change his major from math to teaching. While he would have been a good mathematician, teaching was what he really loved, a gift that has truly blessed and benefitted thousands over the years.

Sometimes when the elders had business on the coast and we were alone at the house, we tampered with an old army radio from the war. A length of barbed wire that stretched from the house to one of the coconut trees served as an antenna. The night we were trying to find a station through all the static, we had a joyful surprise when the familiar sound of the Mormon Tabernacle Choir came on. It took us home for a few minutes, but then we knew where our real home was the moment the static returned. This old home was also the place we caught hold of the language and the thrill of being able to communicate with the village people in their own language.

Things never got perfectly smooth with a couple of the elders, but they eased somewhat as we all continued with our early morning language study by reading and translating the D&C and, working with our students, even offering extra classes after school. There was one old typewriter in the house, and several students wanted to learn how to use it. They patiently waited their turn. I picture them now with devices far advanced from their first lessons.

And so, it went from village to village as we were moved around the mission. We had our inside joke: since we made improvements—the best we could in each place—this must have been part of our calling! One of the pluses for us was living in the villages away from Pesega where mission headquarters and the church school spread out over many acres. It was there where the sister missionaries lived and worked, kind of a village of its own, but with modern facilities. Living as we did, with the people in the villages away from the mission home, was more inconvenient for us, but I feel fortunate we had that experience of knowing the families, eating with them, learning their customs firsthand, hearing their stories, clearing up some of their misconceptions regarding their skin color as a curse, and helping them see the damage of physical abuse to spouses and children. Our constant search for better ways to teach indeed became our new dance.

After our missions, Gene and I made up for lost time. Over the next nearly fifty years, we took every opportunity to dance. Then, suddenly, dancing was taken away again in February of 2001 when Gene collapsed with a brain tumor, leaving him partially paralyzed; we still held hope. After all he had survived—blood poisoning in Samoa, a crushed lung from a head-on collision while coming down Logan Canyon with his father and business acquaintance from a fishing trip—now this. A new challenge, a new dance … and I had to take the lead because Gene couldn't.

Our last dances took place in the hospital when he was in his wheelchair. I would take him through the back hallways, from his hospital bed to the radiation treatments, because there was space and seldom other people there. I could turn the chair in half circles, even full circles, as if we were on the dance floor again.

Those moments were short and bittersweet, but Gene liked them.

On one of those runs through the back hallways, I reminded him of the time we danced across London's Hungerford Bridge on a freezing cold night over the Thames River. We had taken the students on our study abroad program to a play at the National Theatre. During the performance, the weather changed drastically to bitter cold wind and rain. The students rushed ahead to shelter in the Tube station, but Gene and I lingered a bit when we heard a young man playing his saxophone partway across the bridge. This busker was playing one of "our" songs. Irresistible! We looked at each other and danced all the way to the other side. As we dropped a five-pound note in the young man's instrument case, all three of us were happy.

Many years later, after he was gone, one of Gene's old basketball teammates told me that the summer before Gene asked me out, they had been driving back from California when Gene told him he was going to marry me. Of course, he had to ask me out first, he said. And that's how we ended up at the Hello Dance. I'm still learning, even now, new things like this, little stories, about how deeply he loved me. This boy from a farm in Idaho bewitched me, challenged me, believed in me when I didn't believe in myself. He gave me joy that I never dreamed possible and strengthened me through trials that I felt were impossible to survive.

In every way, he was my best partner. I look forward to the next dance when he takes my hand and we dance again and again and again. There can be no heaven without it.